INTO THE THINK TANK
WITH LITERATURE

by Jo Ann Pelphrey

Incentive Publications, Inc.
Nashville, Tennessee

Cover and illustrations by Susan Eaddy
Edited by Jan Keeling

ISBN 0-86530-192-1

TABLE OF CONTENTS

Stories

INTRODUCTION

Contemporary research shows that there has been a breakdown in the natural development of children's thinking skills. This book uses literature in a non-threatening way to lead children to higher levels of thinking and communication skills.

Parents and teachers may use the activities in this book with individual children, small groups, or with entire classes after storytime.

General Objectives:
1. To expose children to various forms of literature.
2. To enhance reading comprehension.
3. To stimulate higher levels of thinking.
4. To boost vocabulary and word usage skills.
5. To foster imagination and creativity.
6. To build positive self-images in a non-threatening atmosphere.

Strategies:

For each story or rhyme you plan to present, select questions and activities from this book that will meet your students' needs and interests. Then read the story aloud to the children. Encourage the children to share thoughts with one another.

The selected questions and activities should be used in a non-critical way. Show respect for each child's ideas; the process of discussion is more important than the product.

It is well to remember that this book is intended to provide the parent or teacher and child with a method of improving and exchanging ideas. Not all questions and answers need to be planned. In a non-critical atmosphere, questions and answers will flow naturally.

PLANNING THE LESSONS

Selection of Materials

Your students' interests and levels of knowledge and experience must be considered in your selection of materials. For kindergarten classes, preparation is particularly important. If you must stop to find something or walk across the room to get something, you will have lost your students' attention.

On page 156 is a bibliography of the modern stories used in this book. The fairy tales and nursery rhymes are, of course, tales and rhymes that have been told and retold and printed in countless versions. Select the versions that are readily available and most familiar to (and beloved by) you. Please note that it may be necessary to search out the longer versions of a few of the nursery rhymes (such as "The Three Little Kittens") in order to use the activities and questions effectively.

Presentation of Materials

There are many ways to introduce a story or rhyme:

1. The class sits "Indian style" in a magic circle on the floor or rug. As the story is read or told, the book is held so the children may enjoy the pictures. You can use an object to interest the children in the story. For example, hold a handful of pebbles and say, "Pebbles like these helped a little lost boy and girl find their way home. Do you know the name of the story?"

2. The story may sometimes be told using a flannelboard. A flannelboard can be made by covering a piece of cardboard with flannel (use two pieces of cardboard for extra durability) and binding the edges with colored tape. Story pictures may be colored, cut out, laminated, and backed with flannel or velcro. It's a good idea to keep manila folders of flannelboard story pictures in your files.

3. Children need to be involved in the story. They may make the "trip-trap" noise of the Billy Goats Gruff or sing the song of the Gingerbread Man. They can do body movements for "Hickory, Dickory, Dock," "Two Little Blackbirds," "Bear Hunt," and other old favorites.

4. It is fun for the storyteller to dress up like a storybook character and tell the story from that character's point of view.

5. The video industry has many filmed folktales on the market that are readily available at the school or public library.

6. Most stories have a beginning, middle, and an ending. The sequencing approach can be especially important if the teacher or parent wants the children to begin composing stories.

7. A very old storytelling method is "chalk talk," where the story is "drawn," either on the blackboard or chart paper, as it is told.

8. Children take delight in stories told with puppets. A table turned on its side can be used for a stage.

The content of the story helps determine the responses of the children. Some stories lend themselves to strengthening listening skills and lengthening interest spans while others naturally lead to active involvement.

INDEPENDENT AND GROUP STUDY

After the story is presented, the teacher leads a discussion by asking questions and accepting with enthusiasm all reasonable answers. During the latter part of kindergarten and first grade years, after the children have learned to work together, the teacher may begin to give the questions, orally or in written form, to a team of two to four students. The students should be given the opportunity to develop several responses. This usually requires 10 to 15 minutes.

In the second and third grades, the children may read the story silently, then independently work on designated activity sheets. After a given amount of time, the students regroup in order to share their work.

Children's interest and ability levels may be determined through observation of their responses to the materials and activities presented. (Benjamin Bloom's *Taxonomy of Education* will serve as an excellent teacher resource for this type of observation.) Lessons can then be planned to better meet both individual and group needs. A wide range of questions to meet varying student needs has been included in the lesson plans in this book.

FOLLOW-UP ACTIVITIES

Artwork

A variety of art media may be used to illustrate the story. You may have the children make finger, sack, or stick puppets; create a TV screen from a shoe box with dowel rollers (draw the story in sequence to roll on the screen); model objects from the story with items such as modeling clay, toothpicks, buttons, and sugar cubes; and try other art projects that can enhance a story.

Hands-On Enrichment Experiences

Plan many direct hands-on experiences after discussing the stories. For example, have children sort small, medium, and large items after reading stories such as "Goldilocks and the Three Bears" or "The Three Billy Goats Gruff," or have them classify city and country sounds pictures after enjoying "The City Mouse and the Country Mouse."

Games

Adapt games such as *Concentration*, commercial and teacher-made card games, and memory games so that they feature storybook characters.

Puppet Theater

A curtain on a string or a chair turned over makes a fine puppet stage. Children may take turns presenting and watching storybook character puppets.

Library Center

Provide time for children to reread the story and enjoy the pictures as a culminating experience in a relaxed and unhurried setting. If possible, set up these activities as free-choice centers or learning stations and allow the children to make their own choices. (Some rules will probably be necessary, such as "No more than four students in a center at one time," and "Students may not go to the same center twice in a row.")

INTERACTION OF STUDENTS

Many educational materials now in use emphasize rote thinking skills and fail to encourage thinking as a developmental process. It has been proven that children learn better from their peers and by doing than from lectures or question-and-answer worksheets. The activities in this book have been planned to encourage learning by doing and through shared experiences.

Discussion

The entire group may return to the storytime circle to share their work. At this time spontaneous verbal input is of the utmost importance. The teacher's job is primarily secretarial, listing the ideas on the board or chart. The teacher is also a guide, encouraging brainstorming, and a cheerleader, motivating students to deeper levels of thinking.

Dramatics and Role-Playing

With just a few props the children can enjoy dramatics. For example, steps made from blocks, a small table, and grocery bag masks are all that are needed for "The Three Billy Goats Gruff." Posterboard decorated to feature storytime characters and with circles cut out for head and hands can provide the only props necessary for a wonderfully creative human puppet presentation.

Telling the story in "rounds" is fun. One child begins the story. When the teacher rings a bell, the next child picks up the story, and so forth.

Debates

Debating can be another way of learning, especially for the older primary child. A question for debate may be something like: Does Jack have a right to take the giant's harp, hen, and bag of money in the story "Jack And The Beanstalk"?

THINKING SKILLS ASSESSMENT

Keep a log of each student's responses. Make a check after the student's name when he or she volunteers an answer. By using a chart like the one below you can readily assess the student's level of thinking skills development.

Name	Productive Thinking	Planning	Communication	Forecasting/Decision Making
Mary				
John				
Sue				

Here are a few ways to keep the whole class involved in oral discussions:

- Call on non-volunteers regularly.
- Ask students to elaborate on what someone else has said.
- Have students give "thumbs up" signals if they agree with comments made, "thumbs down" signals if they disagree.

Ask open-ended questions to allow for expansion of reasoning skills. Certain key words such as "define," "explain," "compare," and "summarize" may be used to trigger responses that involve higher-level thinking skills (see page 13 for a more complete list of these "trigger words").

THINKING SKILLS AREAS

Research by Lewis Leon Thurstone, J.P. Guilford, and Calvin Taylor shows that some important thinking skills are not fully developed through the use of the usual academic exercises. Productive Thinking, Planning, Communication, and Forecasting and Decision-Making are thinking skills that require more than rote exercises to become fully developed.

Productive Thinking

Productive thinkers come up with many and varied ideas. They often solve problems in unique or unusual ways.

1. The student expresses many ideas (not necessarily of the highest quality) and ideas flow freely. A productive thinker notices details.

2. The student expresses a variety of responses, usually original, often contrary to popular opinion.

3. The student can take a concept and expand it, building or developing a basic idea.

Planning

Planners consider details, are sensitive to problems, and consider materials, time, and manpower when coming up with solutions.

1. The student can organize materials, time, and resources to meet the problem.

2. The planner is sensitive to problems that may arise.

3. The student can explain what he or she wants to do and can follow through with the activity in an orderly manner.

Communication

Communicators are not only able to speak so that others understand, but are also good listeners.

1. The student has a rich vocabulary of "describing" words. He or she categorizes, compares, and associates cor.cepts easily.

2. The student can express his or her own feelings, and also has the capacity to understand others' feelings.

Forecasting/Decision-Making

Forecasters / Decision-Makers understand "cause and effect." They are able to make decisions and judgments by weighing alternatives.

1. The student predicts future events.

2. The student can make decisions and give reasons for his or her choices.

3. The student can make judgments when given information.

WORDS ASSOCIATED WITH HIGHER-LEVEL THINKING SKILLS

Productive Thinking

Define	Name
Describe	Explain
Identify	Select
List	Categorize

Planning

Change	Relate
Compute	Outline
Demonstrate	Combine
Prepare	Design
Solve	Construct
Explain	Analyze
Estimate	Contrast

Communication

Interpret	Illustrate
Differentiate	Discuss
Distinguish	Rewrite
Compare	

Forecasting / Decision-Making

Defend	Translate
Predict	Summarize
Criticize	Decide
Justify	Solve
Support	Critique
Conclude	Debate

NURSERY RHYMES

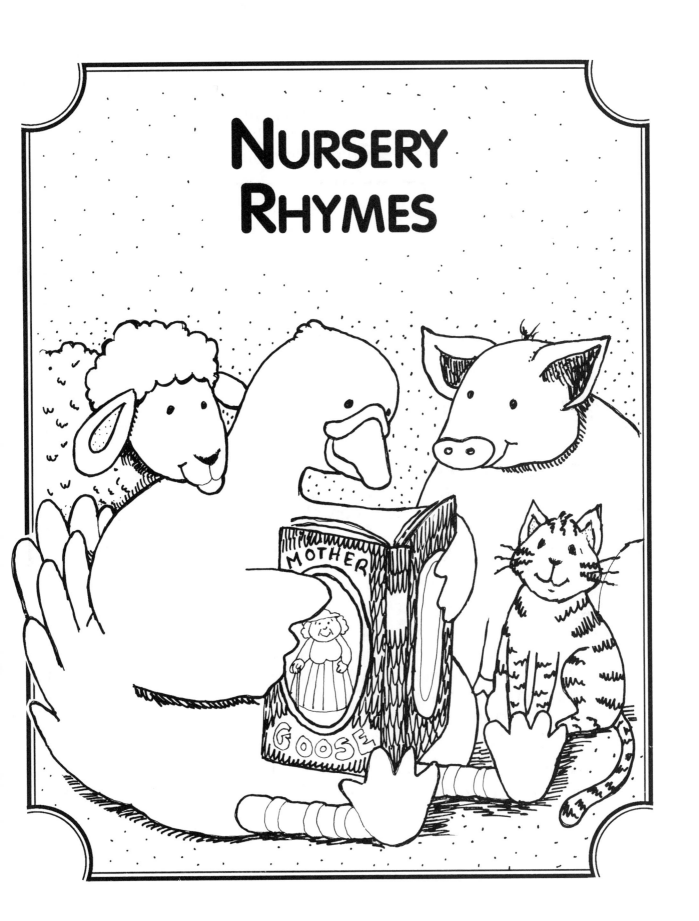

BAA BAA BLACK SHEEP

Baa! Baa! Black sheep, have you any wool?
Yes, sir, yes, sir, three bags full.
One for the master and one for the dame,
And one for the little boy who lives in the lane.

PRODUCTIVE THINKING

The sheep gives wool. What do you have that is made of wool?

Name the steps in making wool. Begin with shearing the sheep.

PLANNING

Make up other verses such as "Cluck, cluck, red hen, have you any eggs," "Moo, moo, brown cow," "Oink, oink, pink pig," etc.

COMMUNICATION

Which farm animal do you think is the most important to people?

FORECASTING/DECISION-MAKING

What if the farm animals went on strike and would not give any wool, eggs, milk, etc.? Write a story about this.

If you were a farmer and could have only one animal, which one would you choose?

FOLLOW-THROUGH ACTIVITIES

- Make a paper mat: Fold a piece of construction paper in half. At one-inch intervals, mark straight parallel lines from the folded edge to within one inch of the opposite edge. Cut along these lines, then unfold the paper. Cut one-inch strips from other pieces of paper in various colors. Weave these strips in and out of the first piece of paper to make your mat.

- Feel various textures of materials: terry cloth, plastic, cotton, corduroy, satin, etc. Use scraps of these materials in a collage.

DING DONG BELL

> *Ding dong bell, Pussy's in the well,*
> *Who put her in? Little Johnny Green.*
> *Who pulled her out? Big John Stout.*
> *What a naughty boy was that*
> *To try to drown little Pussy cat!*

PRODUCTIVE THINKING

Do cats know how to swim?

Name some more naughty things that Johnny Green might do.

PLANNING

How did Johnny Green get the cat in the well?

How did Big John Stout pull her out?

COMMUNICATION

Which one would you rather have for a friend, Johnny Green or Johnny Stout? Why?

FORECASTING/DECISION-MAKING

After Johnny Stout got the cat out, what do you think he did?

FOLLOW-THROUGH ACTIVITIES

- Johnny got his water from a well. Draw a picture showing how we get our water.
- Make a model of a well using blocks, sugar cubes, etc.

HICKORY, DICKORY DOCK

> *Hickory, Dickory Dock;*
> *The mouse ran up the clock;*
> *The clock struck "One,"*
> *The mouse ran down;*
> *Hickory, Dickory Dock.*

PRODUCTIVE THINKING

Why do you think the mouse chose the clock for a home?

PLANNING

How could a mouse cross a room without touching the floor?

COMMUNICATION

How do you think the mouse felt when the clock began to strike?

FORECASTING/DECISION-MAKING

Make up other verses saying the clock struck two, the clock struck three, etc.

Do you think the mouse moved? Make up a story in which the mouse is looking for a new home.

FOLLOW-THROUGH ACTIVITIES

- Look in catalogs. Find as many different clocks as you can.
- Draw as many different kinds of clocks as you can.
- Design your own clock.
- Hide a ticking timer somewhere in the room. Select a student to search for the "clock"; the searcher has "x" minutes to find it before the bell rings.

HUMPTY DUMPTY

Humpty Dumpty sat on a wall,
Humpty Dumpty had a great fall;
All the King's horses and all the King's men,
Couldn't put Humpty Dumpty together again.

PRODUCTIVE THINKING

Where else could Humpty Dumpty have sat?

Why couldn't Humpty Dumpty be put back together?

PLANNING

What do you think the King's horses and King's men did to fix Humpty Dumpty?

Why did Humpty Dumpty fall off the wall?

COMMUNICATION

How did Humpty Dumpty feel when he fell off the wall?

How did the King's men feel when they couldn't help him?

FORECASTING/DECISION-MAKING

If Humpty Dumpty had been a hard-boiled egg, would he have broken when he fell?

If Humpty Dumpty had had his seatbelt on, would he have fallen?

FOLLOW-THROUGH ACTIVITIES

- Carefully break off the top third of an egg, remove the yolk and white, and draw a face on the remaining hollow eggshell. Plant grass seed in the shell to grow "hair."

- Crush eggshells and glue them to a "touch picture." (Examples: Use the shells for leaves on a tree, scales on a fish, etc.)

- Think of a good nutritious breakfast. Share with the class your favorite recipe using eggs.

JACK BE NIMBLE

> *Jack be nimble, Jack be quick,*
> *Jack jumped over the candlestick.*
> *Jack jumped high, Jack jumped low.*
> *Jack jumped over and burned his toes.*

PRODUCTIVE THINKING

What does it mean to be nimble?

What sport could Jack play well because he is nimble and quick?

PLANNING

How did Jack learn to jump so quick and so high?

COMMUNICATION

How do you think Jack felt when everyone in the village talked about his talent?

FORECASTING/DECISION-MAKING

What else might Jack jump over?

What if Jack doesn't want to jump anymore? Make up a story about this.

FOLLOW-THROUGH ACTIVITY

- Play "Build a house with a rope." Start with two people holding a rope on the ground. They should lift the rope slowly as others jump over it. If one person misses, the rope is lowered back to the ground. A variation of this game calls for shaking the rope like a snake. The person bitten (touched) by the snake must take the end of the rope.

LITTLE BO PEEP

Little Bo Peep lost her sheep
And can't tell where to find them.
Leave them alone and they'll come home,
Bringing their tails behind them.

PRODUCTIVE THINKING

How could Little Bo Peep have lost her sheep?

Where do you think the sheep could be?

What other animals might Bo Peep be watching in the pasture?

PLANNING

How could Little Bo Peep have kept track of her sheep?

If you were Little Bo Peep, how would you get the sheep to come back?

COMMUNICATION

How did Little Bo Peep feel when she lost the sheep?

How will she feel when she sees the sheep come home wagging their tails?

FORECASTING/DECISION-MAKING

Will Little Bo Peep get to watch the sheep again?

Do you think the sheep will come back by themselves?

FOLLOW-THROUGH ACTIVITIES

- Make some name tags for the sheep so they can be identified.
- Make a model of a sheep. Use an empty spool or empty toilet paper roll for the body. Glue on cotton balls to make the sheep's wool.

LITTLE JACK HORNER

Little Jack Horner sat in a corner,
Eating a Christmas pie.
He put in his thumb and pulled out a plum
And said, "What a good boy am I."

PRODUCTIVE THINKING

What other kind of pie could Jack be eating?

Why was Jack sitting in the corner?

PLANNING

How would Jack eat his pie if he had good manners?

If you were Jack's mother, what would you do?

COMMUNICATION

Have you ever had to sit in a corner for misbehavior? Do you remember the time?

Why do you think Jack said he was a good boy?

FORECASTING/DECISION-MAKING

Do you think Jack was a good boy? What are some good table manners?

FOLLOW-THROUGH ACTIVITIES

- Make a recipe for "Christmas pie."

- Name or draw foods that are especially popular at Christmastime.

- Triangles, rectangles, and squares have corners. Cut these shapes from construction paper, and use them to build a picture.

LITTLE MISS MUFFET

Little Miss Muffet sat on a Tuffet,
Eating some curds and whey.
There came a great spider and sat down beside her,
And frightened Miss Muffet away.

PRODUCTIVE THINKING

What else could Little Miss Muffet sit on while she was eating?

Are spiders dangerous?

PLANNING

What should Little Miss Muffet have done when she saw the spider?

COMMUNICATION

Did Little Miss Muffet see the spider before she sat down?

Do you think the spider would have hurt her?

FORECASTING/DECISION-MAKING

Change the story. Let Little Miss Muffet share her curds and whey with the spider.

FOLLOW-THROUGH ACTIVITIES

- Take soft clay or other "sculpting" materials and make a spider.

- Design some chairs or stools for Little Miss Muffet to sit on.

- Dunk a short string into thick tempera paint. Pull the string over the surface of a piece of paper. Vary colors to make a beautiful spider web.

MARY HAD A LITTLE LAMB

Mary had a little lamb, its fleece was white as snow.
Everywhere that Mary went the lamb was sure to go.
He followed her to school one day, which was against the rules.
It made the children laugh and play to see the lamb at school.

PRODUCTIVE THINKING

What other pet could Mary have had?

Think of a name for Mary's white lamb.

PLANNING

How could Mary have kept the lamb from coming to school?

Where could Mary have put the lamb until school was out?

COMMUNICATION

Why do you think the lamb followed Mary all the time?

Has a dog ever come into your school building? Tell about what happened.

FORECASTING/DECISION-MAKING

Why did the children laugh when they saw the lamb in the doorway?

FOLLOW-THROUGH ACTIVITIES

- Sing a song about Mary's lamb. In your song have Mary go somewhere other than school.

- Draw a picture to show what could have happened after the lamb went into the school.

- Pantomime this nursery rhyme with a friend.

THE NORTH WIND

*The North Wind doth blow
And we shall have snow,
And what will poor robin do then, poor thing.
She'll sit in the barn
To keep herself warm,
And hide her head under her wing, poor thing.*

PRODUCTIVE THINKING

What kind of weather might the North Wind bring us?

The robin is a bird that stays with us all winter. Name birds that migrate.

PLANNING

Draw a winter picture. What do you do to get ready for winter?

COMMUNICATION

Give two reasons we should care for the birds during the winter.

Have you ever felt cold? Describe what it feels like.

FORECASTING/DECISION-MAKING

Where else could the robin go to try to keep warm?

If you were going out in the cold, what would you do to keep warm?

FOLLOW-THROUGH ACTIVITIES

- Make a pinwheel: Cut a square from construction paper. Fold the square in half by bringing opposite corners together. Unfold, then fold in half again by bringing the remaining two corners together. Unfold, then cut along the creases to within an inch of the center (there will be four cuts in all). Fold four of the corners to the center to make a pinwheel shape and pin to the end of a straw.

- Draw a picture of the robin in the springtime.

- Play blow ball: Players are at each end of a table. A table tennis ball is placed in the center of the table. Each player huffs and puffs, trying to blow the ball off the opponent's end of the table.

OLD KING COLE

Old King Cole was a merry old soul,
A merry old soul was he.
He called for his pipe, he called for his bowl,
And he called for his fiddlers three.

PRODUCTIVE THINKING

What did the King want to do when he was merry? What three things did he ask for?

What songs do you think the King asked the fiddlers to play?

PLANNING

If you were the King's servant, what would you put in the bowl?

COMMUNICATION

Would the King still be merry if the servant could not find his pipe or bowl? How would the story end if the fiddlers were not in the courtyard?

FORECASTING/DECISION-MAKING

What would you take to the King if you could not find what he asked for?

FOLLOW-THROUGH ACTIVITIES

- Draw or name some things that make you merry.
- Old King Cole loved music. Make a felt-tip pen "dance" along a piece of paper to music. Make dots with the pen in time to the music.

PAT-A-CAKE

Pat-A-Cake, Pat-A-Cake, baker's man,
Bake me a cake as fast as you can.
Pat it and prick it and mark it with a B,
And put it in the oven for Baby and me.

PRODUCTIVE THINKING

What can you buy at a bakery?

Do you think the cake in the poem is more like a cookie or a cake? Why?

PLANNING

What are the steps involved in making cookies? What materials would you need to make your favorite cookies?

COMMUNICATION

What is your favorite cookie?

How would you share the cookie with Baby?

FORECASTING/DECISION-MAKING

Suppose the bakery was closed. What would you and Baby do?

If you had only enough money to buy one thing at the bake shop, what would it be?

FOLLOW-THROUGH ACTIVITY

- Make some "Uncooked Cookies." Mix together equal parts of peanut butter, honey or corn syrup, and confectioners' sugar—use your hands to thoroughly knead the mixture. Shape the dough into cookie shapes and decorate with raisins, nuts, or gumdrops.

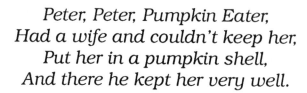

PETER, PETER, PUMPKIN EATER

Peter, Peter, Pumpkin Eater,
Had a wife and couldn't keep her,
Put her in a pumpkin shell,
And there he kept her very well.

PRODUCTIVE THINKING
What are the costs of keeping a wife?

PLANNING
What other materials could Peter have used to build a home?

COMMUNICATION
Do you think Peter's wife liked the pumpkin shell?

FORECASTING/DECISION-MAKING
What would be the advantages and disadvantages of living in a pumpkin shell?

FOLLOW-THROUGH ACTIVITIES
- Draw pumpkins with faces. Use funny shapes for eyes, noses, and mouths. Make some of the faces happy, sad, angry, or scared.

- Make up a story about a pumpkin's life as a Jack-O-Lantern.

PUSSY CAT, PUSSY CAT

> *Pussy Cat, Pussy Cat, where have you been?*
> *I've been to London to visit the Queen.*
> *Pussy Cat, Pussy Cat, what did you there?*
> *I frightened a little mouse under her chair.*

PRODUCTIVE THINKING

How would Pussy Cat get to London? Make up a story about this adventure.

PLANNING

Do you think the palace needs a full-time cat? Make an advertisement to get one.

COMMUNICATION

How do you think Pussy Cat felt when she helped the Queen?

Do you think Pussy Cat would leave London? Why?

FORECASTING/DECISION-MAKING

If you were the Queen, how would you reward Pussy Cat?

Do you think Pussy Cat ever returned to London for a visit?

FOLLOW-THROUGH ACTIVITIES

- Draw a picture of the cat's visit.

- Pretend you are going to visit the queen. What would you say? What would you do?

RIDE A COCK-HORSE
TO BANBURY CROSS

Ride a cock-horse to Banbury Cross,
To see a fine lady upon a white horse.
With rings on her fingers
And bells on her toes,
She shall have music wherever she goes.

PRODUCTIVE THINKING

What else do you think a person might see at Banbury Cross?

What do we use horses for besides riding?

What colors can horses be?

PLANNING

Design a dress for the fine lady to wear.

Plan a carnival for Banbury Cross. How will you tell people about it?

COMMUNICATION

Have you ever ridden your rocking horse to a pretend land? Tell about it.

FORECASTING/DECISION-MAKING

Where could the lady put the bells other than on her toes?

FOLLOW-THROUGH ACTIVITIES

- Design some rings for your fingers from scrap materials.

- Act out the many ways a horse can move: gallop, trot, canter, run, walk, and jump.

Sing A Song Of Sixpence

Sing a song of sixpence, a pocket full of rye,
Four and twenty blackbirds baked in a pie.
When the pie was opened the birds began to sing.
Wasn't that a dainty dish to set before the king?
The king was in his counting house, counting out his money;
The queen was in the parlor, eating bread and honey;
The maid was in the garden, hanging out the clothes;
Down flew a blackbird and pecked off her nose.

PRODUCTIVE THINKING
Tell what each person in the rhyme was doing. What do you think the blackbird thought the maid's nose was?

PLANNING
Can you think of a dish fit for the king? How would you make a dish fit for a king?

COMMUNICATION
If you were a king, would you like the blackbird pie? Why or why not?

FORECASTING/DECISION-MAKING
How do you think the king would spend his money?

FOLLOW-THROUGH ACTIVITIES
- Name other things that could be hidden in the pie.
- Draw a picture of the pie.

> *There was an old woman who lived in a shoe.*
> *She had so many children, she didn't know what to do.*
> *She gave them some broth without any bread;*
> *Then she whipped them all 'round and sent them to bed.*

PRODUCTIVE THINKING

Draw the floor plan of the shoe house.

Name some broth the old woman could have given the children.

PLANNING

If you were the old woman, what would you do with all your children?

If having too little space was a problem, what could the children do?

COMMUNICATION

Do you think the old woman was a good mother? Why or why not?

When should mothers whip their children?

FORECASTING/DECISION-MAKING

Suppose the old woman and her family lived in a boat instead of a shoe. Would the story change?

Why did the mother give her children only broth?

What is the best way to discipline misbehaving children?

FOLLOW-THROUGH ACTIVITIES

- Draw a picture of the old woman and her children. What are they doing?

- Name or draw some activities you would do with your own children when you grow up.

THREE LITTLE KITTENS

Three little kittens lost their mittens,
And they began to cry,
Oh, Mother, dear, we sadly fear
Our mittens we have lost.
What? Lost your mittens! You naughty kittens!
Then you shall have no pie.
Meow, meow, meow, meow!
No, you shall have no pie.
Meow, meow, meow, meow!

PRODUCTIVE THINKING

Where could the kittens have lost their mittens? How did they find them?

Why do you think they ate the pie wearing their mittens?

PLANNING

At the end of the poem, Mother smells a rat close by. What do you think will happen next?

COMMUNICATION

When the kittens were sad, they meowed; when they were happy, they purred. How do you show you are happy or sad?

FORECASTING/DECISION-MAKING

What would Mother do if the kittens soiled their mittens? What if they tore them?

Do you think the mother cat was a good mother? Explain your answer.

FOLLOW-THROUGH ACTIVITIES

- Trace your left hand, then your right. Make the outlines into a pair of mittens or gloves. Decorate them.

- The good little kittens were rewarded with pie. Name ways that you are rewarded.

TOM, TOM, THE PIPER'S SON

Tom, Tom, the piper's son,
Stole a pig and away he run!
The pig was eat, and Tom was beat,
And Tom went crying down the street.

PRODUCTIVE THINKING

What foods do we get from a pig?

Who do you think beat Tom?

PLANNING

How do you think Tom caught the pig?

COMMUNICATION

Was Tom's punishment sufficient for his crime?

Why do you think Tom stole the pig instead of getting food another way?

FORECASTING/DECISION-MAKING

If Tom were brought to trial and if you were the judge, how would you have Tom repay the farmer for his pig?

FOLLOW-THROUGH ACTIVITIES

- Draw some places Tom could have run to hide the pig.

- Write a news release on this story. Remember to include what happened, who was involved, when it happened, and where it happened.

- Pretend to be a lawyer. Defend Tom or the owner of the pig.

TWINKLE, TWINKLE, LITTLE STAR

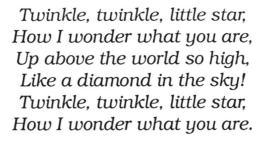

Twinkle, twinkle, little star,
How I wonder what you are,
Up above the world so high,
Like a diamond in the sky!
Twinkle, twinkle, little star,
How I wonder what you are.

PRODUCTIVE THINKING

People have been fascinated by the stars for thousands of years. What do you know about them?

What else is in the sky besides stars?

PLANNING

Why don't we see stars in the daytime?

Make a map of the sky showing the Big Dipper.

How could the North Star help you if you were lost?

COMMUNICATION

Have you ever wished upon a star?

Did your wish come true?

What is peaceful about the stars shining?

Can stars put you to sleep? If so, how?

FORECASTING/DECISION-MAKING

When do we not see any stars in the sky? Why?

Why do some compare a star to a diamond?

FOLLOW-THROUGH ACTIVITY

- Do some research to find out which stars you can see from your part of the world.

FAIRY TALES

THE BREMEN-TOWN MUSICIANS

Productive Thinking

1. Could the animals have found their own food? Where?

2. How does each of the animals (donkey, dog, cat, and rooster) plan to make music?

3. Do you think the animals would have been friends if they hadn't had a common problem?

4. What could each of the animals do to help the others along the journey to Bremen-town?

5. What made the robbers think the attacker was a witch or monster?

6. What kind of welcome did each of the animals give the returning robber?

7. The animals planned to make music with their voices. What else can you use to make music?

8. What are the advantages of being young? Old?

Planning

1. If the donkey could not plow the fields, what could he do?

2. If the dog could not hunt, what could he do?

3. What could the cat do besides chase mice?

4. How did the animals scare the robbers? Can you think of some other way they might have gotten the robbers to leave?

5. If you were one of the robbers, how would you have planned a return trip to the house?

Communication

1.   How do you think it made the donkey feel to hear his master say he (the donkey) was too old to work? Have your feelings ever been hurt?

2.   Do you think the master was sad when the donkey left?

3.   Would the animals have been as happy in Bremen-town as they were in the house?

4.   Who is your favorite musician? Why?

5.   When would the animals have sung happy songs? Sad songs?

Forecasting/Decision-Making

1.   What problems might the donkey, dog, cat, and rooster have living together?

2.   What would the animals have done if they had seen a family inside the house? Finish this story.

3.   What would happen if the owner of the house came back? Finish the story.

4.   If you were the master, what would you do with your animals when they got old?

5.   What parts of this story could be real and what parts must be pretend?

Follow-Through Activities

•   Role-playing: Be a police officer or a TV reporter. What questions would you ask the musicians about the incident with the robbers?

•   Plan how you would have caught the robbers.

•   How many sounds can you make with the various parts of your body? For example: tapping toes, kissing, etc. (The team with the most can record their noises.)

Draw a line from each animal to Bremen-Town,
without crossing any lines along the way.

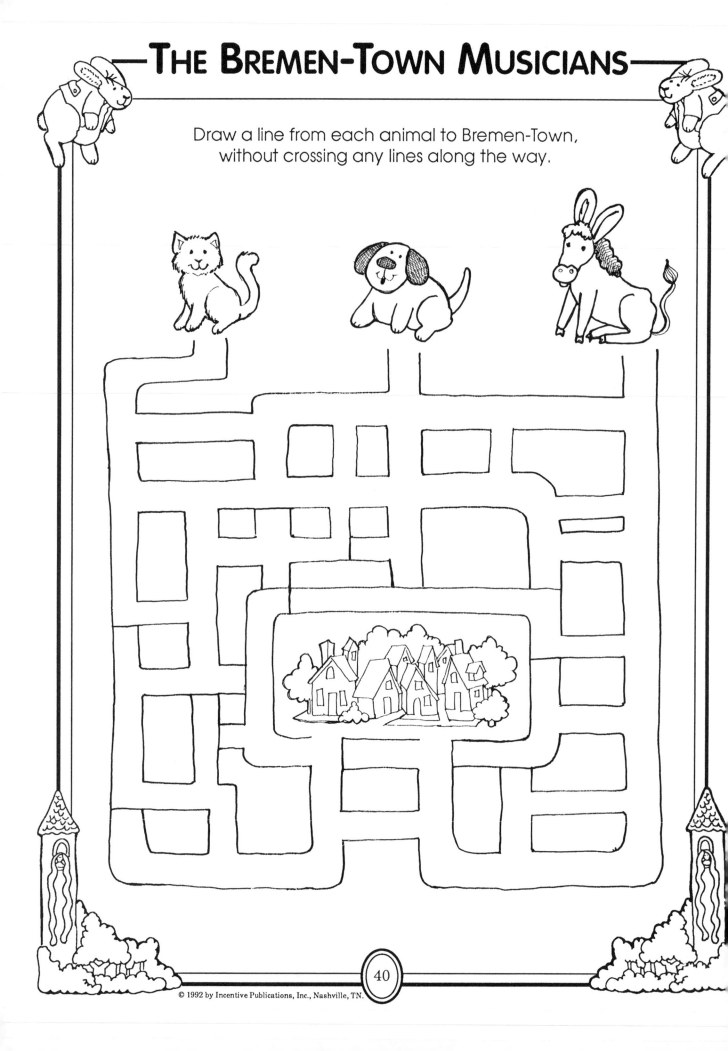

THE BREMEN-TOWN MUSICIANS

Draw a line from each animal to the sound it makes.

A dog says

Quack-quack.

A duck says

Bow-wow.

A chicken says

Oink -oink.

A pig says

Moo-moo.

A cow says

Cluck-cluck.

Productive Thinking

1. Cinderella got her name because one of her chores was "sweeping the cinders." Draw or list Cinderella's other chores.

2. Design a robot that will do a chore you do not like.

3. How did the stepsisters know about the Prince's Ball? Name other ways the Prince could have announced the dance.

4. What did Cinderella see as she walked into the castle?

5. Cinderella's slipper was glass. Draw or list as many "foot coverings" as you can.

Planning

1. Give Cinderella a different name. Explain your choice.

2. The Prince sent a footman over the entire village with the glass slipper. What other ways might the Prince have found Cinderella?

3. Design Cinderella's dress for the ball.

4. Plan the ball. What music will you have? How will you decorate the ballroom? What food will you serve?

Communication

1. What do you think Cinderella did when the stepsisters and stepmother treated her so badly?

2. What three things would you like the Fairy Godmother to do for you?

3. Pretend you are interviewing Cinderella. What questions would you ask her? Interview the stepmother; then interview Cinderella's stepsisters.

4. How do you think Cinderella felt when the stepsisters tried to get their big feet into the slipper?

5. Why did the Fairy Godmother let Cinderella go to the ball?

Forecasting/Decision-Making

1. Predict what would take place after Cinderella and the Prince were married.

2. Most fairy tales portray stepmothers as evil characters. Suppose the stepmother was a kind, loving person. Create a new story.

3. Name three qualities a good mother has that Cinderella's stepmother did not have.

4. Would you like to get married someday? What will your wedding be like?

Follow-Through Activities

• Game: Have the children take off their shoes and mix them up. One child, the prince's messenger, tries to match the correct shoes for each child. (This activity works best with a group of eight to ten children.)

• Use a pretend fairy godmother's magic wand. Change children into various animals or people. Have them act out their roles.

CINDERELLA

Design Cinderella's dress for the ball, completing the picture.

CINDERELLA

Number the pictures to put these means of transportation in order from the fastest to the slowest way to get to the ball. Color the pictures.

BOAT

CAR

HORSEBACK

WALKING

AIRPLANE

TRAIN

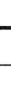

THE CITY MOUSE
AND
THE COUNTRY MOUSE

Productive Thinking

1.   Name some animals that are larger than a mouse. Name some that are smaller.

2.   The city mouse did not like the country food. Compare city food and country food.

3.   What are some city noises that might scare the mice? What noises in the country might alarm them?

4.   List some "picture" words to describe the country. List some "picture" words for the city.

5.   Name some enemies of mice.

6.   How do mice protect themselves?

Planning

1.   What could the mice have done in the country for fun?

2.   Estimate the time it took the mice to get to the city.

3.   What could the city mouse have done so he could have enjoyed his delicious meal?

4.   If you were the country mouse going to the city again, what would you take?

5.   If you were the city mouse making a return visit to the country, what would you take?

Communication

1. The city mouse went to visit his cousin. Have you ever been to visit a cousin or other relatives? Tell about it. Would you like to live there?

2. Why did the country mouse not want to spend even one night with the city mouse?

3. If you were a mouse, would you rather be the city mouse or the country mouse?

4. What does it mean to live in peace?

Forecasting/Decision-Making

1. The city mouse stayed just long enough to eat. If he had stayed longer, would he have liked it better? What could he and his cousin have done to be adventurous? Make up a story about them.

2. Be the city mouse. Try to convince your country cousin to stay longer.

3. How can the two cousins get together again since neither mouse likes the other's home?

4. Would the country mouse have liked the city better if he had visited during the day?

Follow-Through Activities

• Game: Play charades. Make city and country sounds. Guess what they are.

• Make classroom murals of the city and country.

THE CITY MOUSE
AND
THE COUNTRY MOUSE

Cut out the circles.

Put animals in order from smallest to largest.

Decide which animals are "country animals," and put them in a group.

Which animals are sometimes found in the city? Put them in a group.

Are any of these animals not found in the country *or* in the city?

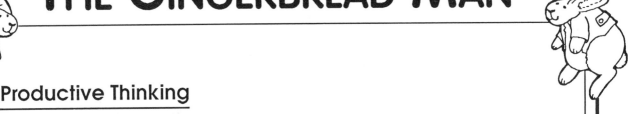

THE GINGERBREAD MAN

Productive Thinking

1. Why did the little old lady decide to make gingerbread?

2. Tell how she made the Gingerbread Man.

3. Name as many kinds of cookies as you can.

4. Why could the Gingerbread Man run faster than the old man and woman?

5. The old man, old woman, and the bear wanted to eat the Gingerbread Man. What did the rabbit want to do with him?

6. The fox could not outrun the Gingerbread Man, but he outsmarted him. Tell about it.

7. Name some animals the Gingerbread Man could probably outrun. Name others that could outrun him.

Planning

1. What other shapes could the little old lady have used for her cookies?

2. Design some gingerbread cookies of your own.

3. Draw a map showing the Gingerbread Man's trip from the oven to the fox's mouth.

4. In what other ways could the Gingerbread Man get across the river?

5. Discuss this statement: The fox had a plan all along for catching the Gingerbread Man.

Communication

1. Be a reporter. Get the story firsthand from each of the characters: the old lady, the old man, the bunny, the bear, and the fox.

2. The Gingerbread Man felt very confident as he ran so fast. Do you think he was ever afraid of the fox?

3. Have you ever been in a situation that seemed to be "trouble" and you thought you should run from it? Tell about it. (Or maybe your friend did something you knew was wrong. How did you feel? What did you do?)

4. What desserts do you think are delicious?

Forecasting/Decision-Making

1. What do you think made the Gingerbread Man come to life?

2. Suppose the Gingerbread Man could swim. How would the story change? Finish it.

3. Maybe the Gingerbread Man ran along the riverbank. Would the story have changed? Would the fox still have caught him? Make up another adventure.

4. If the little old man had caught the Gingerbread Man, how would the story have changed?

Follow-Through Activities

•   Make a dough-like material to mold a gingerbread man. Stir together 4 cups flour, 2 cups salt, 4 tablespoons cream of tartar, 2 tablespoons oil, and 4 cups water (may add food coloring to water). Cook; stir constantly until stiff. Let cool; knead. Store in plastic bags or a plastic container.

•   Fold long sheets of paper to make paper dolls. Cut out dolls. Decorate by adding glasses, curly hair, etc.

Finish the Gingerbread Man.

THE GINGERBREAD MAN

Draw a line from each animal to its product.
(Its "product" is what it gives us.)

© 1992 by Incentive Publications, Inc., Nashville, TN.

THE GOLDEN GOOSE

Productive Thinking

1. The little boy was named Simpleton because everyone thought he was simple. Some people receive names because of the type of work they do. Example: Miller might have milled flour. Think of other names that may have come from traits or occupations.

2. One son cut his arm and the second son cut his leg. How would you have treated these accidents?

3. Not only were the goose's feathers made of gold, but they had magic power. What was it?

4. Simpleton made the king's daughter laugh without trying. Explain how.

5. Estimate how many barrels might have been in the cellar. How many loaves of bread do you think the hungry man could eat in a day?

6. The king said Simpleton must find a ship that would sail on both land and water. What was the ship called?

Planning

1. The two older sons would not share their lunch with the little old man, and he caused them to have an accident. What would have happened if they had given the old man something to eat?

2. The king promised his daughter's hand in marriage to anyone who could make her laugh. Name some things that might have made her laugh.

3. The king did not want Simpleton for a son-in-law, so he gave him some difficult tasks to perform. Name the three tasks. Think of some more tasks the king could have given Simpleton.

4. Design a ship for Simpleton that will travel on both land and water.

5. If you were King Simpleton, how would you reward the little old man?

Communication

1. The little old man had magical power. What would you want him to do for you?

2. If you were Father, would you let Simpleton try his luck chopping wood? Why or why not?

3. The old man left a treasure in the trunk of the tree for Simpleton because he shared his lunch. How do you think Simpleton felt when he saw the golden goose?

4. If you were Simpleton, would you be glad everyone was sticking to your goose? Why didn't it bother Simpleton?

5. Simpleton tried to find the old man so that he could help him. He was disappointed when he could not find him. Have you ever been disappointed when things did not go the way you had hoped, only to find things actually turned out better in the end?

Forecasting/Decision-Making

1. Did Simpleton stick to the goose also? How could he put it down?

2. Suppose Simpleton had not wanted to marry the king's daughter. How would the story be different? Finish it.

3. Simpleton married the princess and later became king. Do you think he ever went back to see the little old man in the woods? Make up another adventure about this.

4. What happened to Simpleton's older brothers?

5. Pretend Simpleton found a bag of gold coins in the tree trunk. What would he have done with them? Finish the story.

Follow-Through Activities

• Play Touch Games: Blindfolded players try to match the textures of materials and describe how they feel . . . bumpy, scratchy, smooth, etc.

• Make a "feely box." Put into it plastic models of animals, cards, etc. Let children reach into the box and guess what an object is by feeling it.

• Make a texture picture that a blind person could enjoy.

THE GOLDEN GOOSE

Draw a line to help the golden goose find her nest.

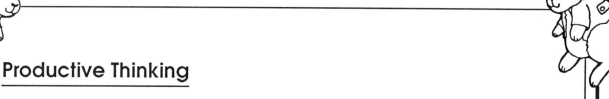

GOLDILOCKS AND THE THREE BEARS

Productive Thinking

1. Goldilocks was given her name because her locks were gold. What would you name her if her hair were brown, red, or black?

2. Goldilocks was going to play in the woods. Mother said, "Stay on the path, don't get lost, and be back by lunchtime." If you were a mom and your child was going to the park, what would you tell your child?

3. Name some hot foods that taste good. Name some cold foods that taste good.

4. What made Goldilocks decide to go inside even when no one was home? What do you think she should have done?

Planning

1. The bears planned to eat oatmeal. Think of another food bears would like to eat. Give the recipe.

2. Suppose Goldilocks told a friend about the "home in the woods." Plan a safe trip to see it.

3. Create a new ending for the story. Begin where Goldilocks awakes.

Communication

1. Goldilocks was lost in the woods. Have you ever felt lost? What did you do?

2. Why was Goldilocks afraid of the bears? Have you ever felt afraid? Tell us about it.

3. How are Little Red Riding Hood's and Goldilocks's experiences alike? Which story did you like best and why?

4. Did Goldilocks make a good decision by running away from the bears? Why?

5.   How do you think Baby Bear felt about the guest? Why?

6.   Father Bear talked in a deep growling voice to express himself. When might you use this voice?

7.   Baby Bear used a little crying voice. When might you use this kind of voice?

Forecasting/Decision-Making

1.   Use information from the story to draw a plan of the bears' house.

2.   Suppose the bears came to visit Goldilocks. What do you think would happen? Make up a story about this event.

3.   Pretend Goldilocks is on trial for "breaking and entering." Would you find her guilty or not guilty? Explain your answer.

Follow-Through Activities

•   Make a papier-mâché porridge bowl. Let it dry. Then paint it.

•   Make trees of the forest. Draw trunks, then dip fingers in various colors of thick tempera paint. Press painted fingers on paper to make autumn leaves.

GOLDILOCKS AND THE THREE BEARS

Draw what you think the three bears would have done
if they had visited the house Goldilocks lived in.

HANSEL & GRETEL

Productive Thinking

1. Hansel secretly gathered pebbles to drop so he and Gretel could find their way home. Why did this plan work? The second time Hansel and Gretel went into the forest, they took only their allotted slice of bread. This time Hansel dropped the crumbs of bread so he and Gretel could find their way home. Why didn't this plan work?

2. On the second trip, Hansel and Gretel were taken deeper into the forest where it is dark all the time, trees are big and old, and the air is much colder. Why is it darker and colder in this part of the forest?

3. A duck helped Hansel and Gretel cross the lake for "kindness' sake." Name some things in your life that are done for "kindness' sake" and not for money.

4. Do you know any other stories that have witches in them? Do these witches look alike? Do they act the same? Compare.

Planning

1. Times were hard. The woodcutter's family had very little money. Using the material resources of the thick forest, how could the family have lived better?

2. Hansel and Gretel overheard their stepmother's plan to lose them in the forest because there was not enough food for the whole family. Was this plan a good idea? What else could the parents have done?

3. Describe the gingerbread house. Design your own gingerbread house on paper; then make it. Use an empty pint milk carton. Glue graham crackers on the sides, and make a roof with confectioners' sugar. Now decorate it with a variety of cookies and candies.

4. Why do you think the mean old witch separated Hansel and Gretel?

5. Describe another plan Gretel could have come up with to save her brother's life and hers.

6. If you were going into the woods, what would you take? Why? How would you find your way home?

Communication

1.   While Hansel and Gretel were alone in the forest, they became very scared, so scared that they saw Dragons' tongues in the fire. Have you ever been so afraid that you saw or heard pretend things? Tell about it. What did you do?

2.   Hansel and Gretel comforted each other. How do you think they did this? If your brother or sister was scared, how would you comfort him or her?

3.   Compare the feelings of the stepmother and the father when they saw the children returning from the forest the first time. Why do you think they felt so differently?

4.   Why was the family so much happier at the end of the story than at the beginning?

Forecasting/Decision-Making

1.   What would have happened if the old gray lady had come out carrying a big stick, yelling at Hansel and Gretel about eating her house? Finish the story.

2.   When the wicked witch decided to eat "skinny" Hansel, she asked Gretel to climb into the oven to see if it was hot. What would have happened if Gretel had done as she was told? Finish the story.

3.   Gretel outsmarted the witch and pushed her into the oven. Was this planned ahead of time or did Gretel simply take an opportunity? Explain your answer.

4.   After the witch was dead, why didn't Hansel and Gretel live in the gingerbread house? Pretend they stayed there. Finish the story.

5.   Was the woodcutter a good husband? A good father? Explain your answer.

Follow-Through Activities

•   Place a piece of masking tape (sticky side out) around each child's wrist. Take a nature walk. Let the children pick up items to stick to their nature bracelet.

Hansel & Gretel

Help the kind duck take Hansel and Gretel across the lake.

JACK AND THE BEANSTALK

Productive Thinking

1. Jack climbed the beanstalk to the giant's home in the sky. List or draw other ways he could have gotten there.

2. List as many things as you can that you might find in the sky.

3. Draw a picture of what the giant's house looked like.

4. After eating, the giant always fell asleep. Imagine what he dreamed about.

5. Jack took the beans because they were pretty. List other things that are pretty.

6. The giant knew Jack was there because he could smell him. List or draw things your nose might tell you.

7. Describe in words or draw a picture of the life cycle of the beanstalk.

Planning

1. Jack's mother sent him to town to sell the cow. How could Jack and his mother have kept the cow and started a business with it?

2. The giant had a hen that laid golden eggs. Were the eggs for eating? Make up a special dish for the giant. List the ingredients needed and tell how to make it.

3. The giant's cook hid Jack in a pot. Where else could Jack have hidden?

4. Jack disguised himself when he went back up the beanstalk. List what Jack could have done in the giant's castle.

5. Build a diorama showing the castle, beanstalk, and Jack's house.

Communication

1. How do you think Jack felt when he got to the top of the beanstalk? Draw a picture of the new and different place he saw.

2. Did Jack have the right to take the bag of money from the giant? Explain your answer.

3. Name three things the giant liked to do. List or draw what you like to do.

4. Make a musical of the story. Make up a song for each character: the giant, Jack, Jack's mother, and the cook.

5. Identify three reasons Jack was afraid of the giant.

Forecasting/Decision-Making

1. Suppose Jack had traded the corn for a bicycle. What would have happened?

2. The old man sold his beans. List ways he could have advertised them. Can you think of a "catchy" advertisement that might attract buyers?

3. How much was the corn worth? Name three things Jack could have traded it for that would have helped him become successful.

4. Why was the cook so upset when she heard the giant coming? She hid Jack. What else could she have done?

5. When Jack chopped down the beanstalk, the giant came tumbling down. What did Jack and his mother do with the giant? Was he dead or just knocked out?

6. Was Jack a good or a bad son? Explain your answer.

7. Retell the story making Jack a girl or the giant a kind person.

Follow-Through Activities

•   Write a story: "If I Were a Giant."

•   Collect small containers like baby food jars and punch holes in the lids. Fill with cloves, dried onions, leather, perfume, and other materials with distinct odors. Make two jars of each. Close your eyes and match the containers by smelling.

JACK AND THE BEANSTALK

Draw what you'd like to find at the top of a beanstalk.

THE LION AND THE MOUSE

Productive Thinking

1.   Why do you think the lion is uncomfortable lying in the hot sun? Name some other animals that prefer cool weather.

2.   The lion is a natural enemy of the mouse. List other forest animals and their enemies.

3.   What do most animals do when they meet someone they fear?

4.   The lion is called the "King of the Beasts." How do you think he got this name? Can you make up a story or draw a picture showing how he got this title?

5.   Name as many forest animals as you can from the smallest to the largest.

6.   Some animals eat meat; others are non-carnivorous and eat plants. Name some animals in each group.

Planning

1.   Would the mouse have been safer if he had climbed over the lion's back and tail?

2.   The mouse was careless and almost lost his life. Name some safety rules people sometimes forget when they are careless.

3.   How is the story *The Ant and the Dove* similar to this one? Make up a story about a snake and a bird, or a flea and an elephant.

4.   Design a trap that can catch an animal without killing it.

5.   Give reasons that support this statement: "Animals should not be trapped."

Communication

1. Why was the mouse brave enough to climb on the lion?

2. The mouse must have felt helpless in the lion's paw. Have you ever felt this way in a situation you couldn't change?

3. The lion became careless, too. While he was hunting for food, he didn't notice the hunter's net. What happened?

4. Describe ways hunters can catch animals without killing them.

5. Have you ever had a friend help you in time of need? Tell about it.

6. The lion and the mouse became friends forever. What made them friends at the end of the story?

Forecasting/Decision-Making

1. Are there any other forest animals that could have helped the lion? Tell what each could have done to free him.

2. What if the lion in the story had been an elephant? Would the story change? Would the mouse have been more afraid of him? Why?

Follow-Through Activities

• Use lion, mouse, and hunter puppets. Give a puppet show. (Use empty toilet paper rolls to make puppets. Use a table turned over for a stage with drawn background scenery.)

• Make up a song for the mouse and the lion to sing.

• Make a chart classifying animals – carnivorous (meat eaters) on the left and herbivorous (plant eaters) on the right.

• Name or draw five ways the lion and the mouse were different from each other.

Answers to Puzzle on Page 67:

Across: 1 good, 4 evil, 8 end, 10 one, 12 low, 14 men, 15 ins, 16 wet, 17 aid, 19 he's, 21 fly, 22 ill, 23 evens

Down: 1 get, 2 on, 3 odd, 5 vow, 6 in, 7 let, 9 violence, 11 devil, 13 angel, 17 aft, 18 dye, 19 his, 20 sly

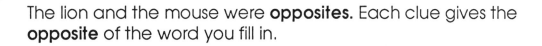

The lion and the mouse were **opposites**. Each clue gives the **opposite** of the word you fill in.

ACROSS

1 Bad
4 Nice
8 Beginning
10 Many
12 High
14 Women
15 Outs
16 Dry
17 Don't help
19 She's
21 Stay on the ground
22 Healthy
23 Odds

DOWN

1 Don't receive
2 Off
3 Even
5 Not promise
6 Out
7 Not allow
9 Peace
11 Angel
13 Devil
17 Fore
18 Bleach (remove color)
19 Hers
20 Not crafty

THE LITTLE RED HEN

Productive Thinking

1.   Name other animals that could have lived with the Little Red Hen.

2.   When the Little Red Hen asked her friends to help her plant the seed, they all said no. What were they doing? Why do you think they would not help?

3.   How could each animal have helped?

4.   What other foods could the Little Red Hen make with the flour?

5.   Design a house where all these animals could live together. Where would each one sleep?

6.   Estimate how long it took the Little Red Hen to get her bread from the grain.

Planning

1.   The cat, dog, and mouse all lived with the Little Red Hen. What chores around the house could each do in order to live happily together?

2.   Tell how the Little Red Hen made the bread.

3.   Draw or tell the story of the flour. Begin with the grain of wheat and end with the bag of flour.

4.   How would the story have changed if the dog, cat, and mouse had helped the Little Red Hen?

Communication

1. Compare the Little Red Hen with her friends.

2. How do you think the Little Red Hen felt when her friends would not help her? Have you ever felt this way? Tell us about it.

3. How did the animals feel when the Little Red Hen would not give them any bread?

4. How do you think the hen felt at the end of the story when she had good hot bread for her little chicks to enjoy? Have you ever felt this way after completing a hard task?

Forecasting/Decision-Making

1. What problem might the Little Red Hen have had with her garden?

2. What other seeds could she have planted to get food for her little ones?

3. Do you think the Little Red Hen should have shared the bread with her friends? Explain your answer.

4. What will happen the next time the Little Red Hen asks the other animals to help?

Follow-Through Activities

• Role play: Make up and act out a story about a duck building a boat while other animals refuse to help. Use the same format as "The Little Red Hen." What happens when the water rises and the animals can't get to the other side?

• Debate the following statement: Little Red Hen had the right not to share her bread.

• Construct a diorama showing the life cycle of a flower.

• Make a picture using seeds and yarn, gluing onto poster board.

THE LITTLE RED HEN

Color the numbered spaces this way:

What do you see?

1. Yellow
2. Red
3. Brown
4. Orange
5. Blue

© 1992 by Incentive Publications, Inc., Nashville, TN.

LITTLE RED RIDING HOOD

Productive Thinking

1.   Everyone loved Little Red Riding Hood, especially Grandmother. Name some things that could have made Little Red Riding Hood "lovable."

2.   The little girl was named Little Red Riding Hood because she wore a red velvet hood all the time. If Grandmother had given her boots, what might her name be?

3.   When Little Red Riding Hood got into the woods, she met a wolf. How would the story have changed if the animal had been a mouse or a bird?

4.   Little Red Riding Hood enjoyed the woods. What did she see, hear, and smell in the woods?

5.   How did Little Red Riding Hood know the person in bed was not her grandmother?

Planning

1.   Design a new coat for the little girl.

2.   The wolf took the short route. Little Red Riding Hood went the long way. Draw a map showing a short route and a long route from your home to school.

3.   The wolf thought of a plan to gobble up both Grandmother and Little Red Riding Hood. Can you think of another plan he might have used?

4.   When Little Red Riding Hood was in trouble, she yelled. What else could she have done?

5.   Change the setting. Have Grandmother live in an apartment house in a big city. Who could be the "villain" instead of the wolf? How would Little Red Riding Hood go to Grandmother's?

Communication

1. Has your grandmother ever given you something very special that you liked as much as Little Red Riding Hood loved her coat? Tell about it.

2. Name as many "picture" words as you can think of to describe the hood.

3. Little Red Riding Hood made the mistake of talking to strangers. What do you think she should have said or done when the wolf talked to her?

4. Do you know any other stories that have wolves in them? Compare them. How are they the same? How are they different?

5. Make up a story (or picture) of a dangerous situation using two or three characters. How do the characters get out of the situation safely?

Forecasting/Decision-Making

1. Mother warned, "Don't stop and play in the woods." What else could she have said or done that would have reminded Little Red Riding Hood to be careful?

2. The wolf answered, "Big ears are all the better to hear you with," "Big eyes are all the better to see you with," and "Big teeth are all the better to eat you with." Is bigger always better? Explain your answer.

3. Did the woodcutter have a right to shoot the wolf? Why or why not?

4. Do you think sending Little Red Riding Hood to Grandmother's house was right or wrong? Explain your answer.

5. If you were a mother and it was dark and your little girl had not come home, how would you feel? What would you do?

6. Will Mother send Little Red Riding Hood to Grandmother's again? If you think so, tell about her next trip. How will it be different?

Follow-Through Activities

• Red is a color that can signal danger. Draw or list things that are red for this reason.

• Draw and color animals found in the forest. Now cut trees from construction paper and hide (camouflage) the animals.

LITTLE RED RIDING HOOD

Choose a healthful meal for Little Red Riding Hood to take to her grandmother.
Draw a line from each healthful food to the basket.

PUSS IN BOOTS

Productive Thinking

1. The miller's sons each received an inheritance: one a mill, another a donkey, and the youngest a cat. Which gift is the most valuable? Which gift is the most useful?

2. As Puss roamed the countryside with his leather boots and bag, what do you think he saw?

3. Why do you think Puss did not tell his master his "get rich" plan?

4. Why do you think Puss in Boots's master trusted him so much that he didn't even ask questions about his plan? Should he have asked or just done as he was told?

5. Puss in Boots wanted his master to have clothes fit for a king. What did these clothes probably look like? What colors were they?

6. Puss promised the mowers working in the field that if they lied and said the land belonged to his master, he would reward them. What do you think Puss gave them?

7. Puss also promised the reapers a reward, too, if they said the land belonged to his master, the make-believe Marquis of Carabas. What did he say and do?

8. Now the rich cat only chases mice for exercise. What do the princess and her new husband do for exercise?

Planning

1. The youngest son received a cat. He thought the only thing he could use it for was food, and its fur for clothing. What else can you do with a cat?

2. Compare the way the cat caught the rabbit to the way he caught the partridge.

3. The cat wanted his master to meet the king's daughter. How would you have arranged their meeting?

4. Why did Puss in Boots want fine clothing for his master? Can you think of another way Puss could have gotten the clothes?

5. Suppose the king had just sent one of his horsemen back with the clothes for Puss in Boots's master. What would Puss have done then? Think of another plan which would lead to the master's meeting the king's daughter.

Communication

1. The cat in the story was a tricky cat. What is the difference between a cat that can do tricks and a tricky cat?

2. Which gift would you rather have—a mill, a donkey, or a cat?

3. How did the king show his pleasure to Puss? What else could the king have done to show his appreciation for the gifts?

4. If the ogre could change you, what animal would you want to become?

5. Describe the cat's character. Would you want someone like him for a friend?

6. Can you make up a new story about the cunning cat Puss in Boots?

Forecasting/Decision-Making

1. Suppose the cat could do tricks. Make up a story about this cat.

2. How do you think the ogre got his castle? Make up a story about this.

3. Puss told everyone the ogre's castle belonged to his master. They feasted on the ogre's food. Was this right? Explain your answer.

4. The king's daughter married the "Marquis" immediately. What do you think will happen when she finds out he was a very poor boy with only a cat?

5. Suppose you brought Puss in Boots to trial. What would you charge? Would you fine him? If so, how?

6. Do you think the youngest son should be tried also?

Follow-Through Activities

- Art Projects:

    1. Take one section of a newspaper. Fold in half. Take the two lower corners, fold up to the center. Turn the extra at the top on both sides down. You've got a hat. Decorate.

    2. Make a picture of the ogre's castle using only scissors, paste, and shapes of construction paper—no pencils or crayons.

Puss In Boots

Draw the fine clothing the king might have given Puss in Boots.

Productive Thinking

1. Say Rapunzel's hair was long enough to reach the ground from a tower that was four stories high; estimate the length of her hair.

2. The witch climbed up Rapunzel's hair. What other ways might she have gotten into the tall tower?

3. What made the prince think Rapunzel's hair was a golden ladder?

4. Why was Rapunzel afraid of the prince?

5. When the prince climbed up the golden hair, he was surprised to see an old witch in the tower. How did he know the witch was mad?

6. The prince leaped out of the tower. How was he hurt? What kept him from being killed?

7. The prince recognized Rapunzel's voice singing from the little cottage in the woods. With your eyes closed, listen to the noises in your classroom. Can you recognize them?

8. Rapunzel's tears of joy fell on the prince's eyes, and he could see again. List or draw some instruments we have that can help us see.

Planning

1. Rapunzel was taken from her parents by a mean old witch. How do you think the witch got her?

2. The witch kept Rapunzel in a tall tower without stairs or doors and only one little window. How did the witch get her up there?

3. Why do you think the witch kept Rapunzel hidden in the tower?

4. Where could the King's son hide so that the witch could not see him?

5. Rapunzel's plan was for the prince to bring silk that she could braid into a ladder so she could climb down. Was this a good plan?

Communication

1. Rapunzel lessened her boredom by singing. What do you do when you are bored?

2. The prince talked with Rapunzel for many hours in the tower. What do you think they talked about?

3. Rapunzel said she knew the prince loved her more than the old witch loved her. How did she know this?

4. Compare Rapunzel's plan to the witch's plan for coming down out of the tower.

5. Compare life in the tower with life in the cottage. How is it the same? Different?

Forecasting/Decision-Making

1. If the witch wanted to come up, she yelled, "Rapunzel, Rapunzel, let down your golden hair." What if Rapunzel had refused to lower her hair?

2. The King's son moved closer to the beautiful song he heard in the forest and was surprised to see a witch climbing up a golden ladder. What would have happened if the prince had ridden closer to the witch? Finish the story.

3. The witch made Rapunzel live in a small cottage in the woods. Which would you rather live in, the tower or the cottage? Explain your answer.

4. The prince took Rapunzel to live in his kingdom. What do you think happened to the witch?

5. If the prince had brought a ladder and some king's soldiers with him, how would the story have changed?

Follow-Through Activities

•   Paint a picture of Rapunzel in the tall tower. (You can add wallpaper paste to tempera paint to simulate oil paint.)

•   Pretend you are the author of "Rapunzel": Where did you get your idea for this story?

•   Blow up a balloon. Set it in a cardboard-strip circle while you design a hairdo and face on it. (Cotton balls, yarn, tempera paint, liquid starch, and curled construction paper strips are a few suggested materials to use.)

RAPUNZEL

Draw some ways Rapunzel could style her hair.
Or think of unusual uses for her long hair and draw them.

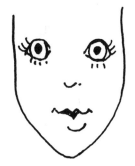
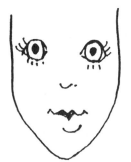

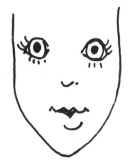

Productive Thinking

1. A miller had a beautiful daughter named Joy. He bragged about her all the time. Once he made up a "tall tale" about her to the king. Do you remember what it was?

2. A funny little man came to help the miller's daughter. What storybook names do we have for these little people?

3. How would the story be different if the beautiful daughter had not gone to the king under false pretenses (he thought she could spin gold)?

4. Name some things made of gold. Why is gold so valuable?

5. Why didn't the king ask Joy to spin gold after she became queen?

6. Why did Rumpelstiltskin ask her to guess his name?

Planning

1. The king had one purpose in meeting the daughter. What was that?

2. The daughter was taken to the tower where she was ordered to spin the straw into gold, and told not to fail the king. What would have happened if she had failed? Finish the story this way.

3. If you were Rumpelstiltskin, what would you ask the girl for in return for spinning straw into gold?

4. What would you ask Rumpelstiltskin to do with his magic powers at your house?

5. What if Rumpelstiltskin hadn't returned the third time? If you were Joy, what would you have done?

6. What do you think the king did with all the gold?

7. For each letter of the alphabet, think of a name that begins with that letter.

Communication

1.   The miller and his daughter had different feelings about meeting the king. What were they, and why did each feel this way?

2.   Draw a picture of the daughter on her way to the palace.

3.   How would you feel if you were Joy in the tower and had three days to spin the gold? What would you do?

4.   Have you ever had a friend do you a favor and then demand something? Tell about it.

5.   Joy was so tired she fell asleep. What do you think she dreamed about?

6.   Why do you think it took the king three days to notice Joy's beauty? If she had met him under different circumstances, might he have noticed her immediately? Make up a story about this.

Forecasting/Decision-Making

1.   If the queen had never thought of the little man's name, what might have happened?

2.   Suppose the queen had told the king about her adventures with the little old man. What would the king have done, especially with the young prince?

3.   The queen rewarded the servant handsomely for telling her the little man's name, Rumpelstiltskin. If you were the queen, what would you have done for the servant?

4.   Do you think Rumpelstiltskin was good or bad? Explain your answer.

Follow-Through Activities

• Pretend you are a reporter: Write a newspaper account of this story.

• Draw or describe how you think Rumpelstiltskin might look.

• Have you ever told a "tall tale"? Write a story or draw a picture of what it was and tell what happened.

RUMPELSTILTSKIN

Create as many words as you can from the letters:

R-U-M-P-E-L-S-T-I-L-T-S-K-I-N

MY NAME IS RUMPELSTILTSKIN

RUMPELSTILTSKIN

Pretend you have Rumpelstiltskin's magic power.
Draw what you will do.

SLEEPING BEAUTY

Productive Thinking

1.   One day while the Queen was walking in the forest, a little fish told her she would soon have a lovely daughter. What other animals in the forest could have told her this?

2.   Name as many kinds of fish as you can.

3.   The baby was named Rosebud. Do you know any other names that sound like a flower's name?

4.   We know only four of the gifts the fairies gave the new baby: virtue, beauty, wealth, new life. Name twelve gifts the fairies could have given her.

5.   How did the twelfth fairy change the wicked curse that would have caused Rosebud to prick her finger and fall dead?

6.   How did the castle become normal again?

Planning

1.   The king invited only twelve fairies because he had only twelve gold plates. How could he have had a thirteenth fairy as a guest, too?

2.   The king ordered all the spindles in his kingdom destroyed. How could he have made sure they were destroyed?

3.   No one could get through the thick hedge of thorns until Prince Charles found a path of flowers. How could the others have gotten through the thorns to the castle?

4.   Plan the wedding feast for Prince Charles and Rosebud: Who will the guests be? How long will it last? What will you serve? How will you decorate the castle?

Communication

1. How did the thirteenth fairy feel? Tell us about her behavior.

2. Have you ever not been invited to a party? How did you feel?

3. What gift would you give the princess if you were a good fairy?

4. Describe the castle during the one hundred years of sleep.

5. How do you think Prince Charles heard about the Castle of Thorns?

Forecasting/Decision-Making

1. How would you have gotten rid of all the spindles?

2. Do you think the old woman who sat spinning at the top of the stairs was the wicked fairy? Explain your answer.

3. How are the stories of *Sleeping Beauty* and *Snow White* alike?

4. Do you think all thirteen fairies were invited to the wedding banquet for Rosebud and Prince Charles?

Follow-Through Activities

- No one has ever seen a real fairy. Draw a picture of how you think fairies would look.

- Play statues: Freeze when a signal is given.

SLEEPING BEAUTY

Draw a picture showing how you think something will change in the next 100 years.

Choose something like transportation, communication, farming, furniture, hospitals, or something else to draw.

SNOW WHITE

Productive Thinking

1. If Snow White had been born with brown or yellow skin, what might her name have been?

2. Snow White's mother wanted a daughter with lips as red as blood, skin as white as snow, and hair as black as a raven. "Red as blood," "white as snow," and "black as a raven" are similes. Make up some similes to go with these phrases: Big as …, mean as …, blue as …, green as …, quiet as …, hard as …, bright as …, shining as …, tall as …, dark as ….

3. Compare the first queen and the second queen. How are they alike and how are they different?

4. Using the content of the story, draw a picture comparing the heights of Snow White and the dwarfs.

5. Snow White named the dwarfs Doc, Dopey, Sneezy, Bashful, Grumpy, Sleepy, and Happy. Why did she choose these names?

6. Why did the dwarfs let Snow White go with the prince?

7. The queen got her wish for a beautiful daughter. Do you know any other stories where wishes come true? Tell about them.

Planning

1. Draw the stages of life of Snow White as she grows from a little baby girl into a beautiful lady.

2. The lovely queen disguised herself as an old lady selling apples. Draw or tell how she did this.

3. The dwarfs thought Snow White was dead. They put her in a glass case with flowers all around it. There she slept. What could the dwarfs have done to awaken her?

4. When the mirror told the queen, "Snow White is much lovelier than you," she became enraged and planned to have Snow White killed. What could the queen have done to make herself more beautiful?

5. The servant told Snow White the queen's plan to harm her. If you were Snow White, how would you have felt, and what would you have done?

Communication

1. Why do you think Snow White was not afraid of the old lady?

2. The seven dwarfs went off to work every morning and came home every evening. Where do you think they worked? What did they do?

3. While Snow White was in the woods, she was not afraid of the birds or animals. She feared the trees. She thought they would grab her. Have you ever been afraid? How did you overcome this fear?

4. The prince asked the dwarfs if he could marry Snow White. Why did they say yes?

5. When during the story did Snow White feel sad, scared, happy?

Forecasting/Decision-Making

1. Why do you think the dwarfs were not afraid of Snow White? How would the story have changed if they had been afraid to go into the bedroom where she slept?

2. The birds tried to chase the old lady away, but Snow White did not understand. If the birds could talk, what would they have said?

3. If one of the dwarfs lifted Snow White and kissed her, would she have awakened? Explain your answer.

4. What do you think happened to the queen? Did the magic mirror tell her Snow White was still the fairest in the land? If so, what did the queen do?

Follow-Through Activities

Make up songs for:
- Snow White to sing as she cleaned the cottage.
- The dwarfs as they worked in the forest.
- The queen when she looked in the mirror.
- The saddened dwarfs when they found Snow White lifeless.
- The prince when he kissed Snow White.

SNOW WHITE

Draw a line to mark a path for Snow White
to follow to the house in the woods.

THE THREE BILLY GOATS GRUFF

Productive Thinking

1.   The three Billy Goats had to cross over the bridge that the troll thought he owned. Think of some other ways the goats could have gotten across the river. List or draw pictures of these ways.

2.   The troll had the reputation of being a "mean old" troll. What traits did he have that made him mean? Name other mean things he might have done.

3.   Make a bridge using sticks and modeling material or other scrap material.

4.   Draw or make a list of some activities the smallest goat could do that the largest goat could not do. What could the largest goat do that the smallest goat could not do?

5.   The old troll thought he owned the bridge. Who does own the bridge? Who takes care of the bridge's repairs, painting, etc.?

6.   How were the goats different from one another?

Planning

1.   When the smallest goat had a problem ("I'm going to come up and eat you"), he passed the problem on to his brother. List some answers he could have given the troll, or draw pictures of things he could have done.

2.   Do you think the old troll did or did not like the "trip-trap" sound? How could this noise have been softened or eliminated?

3.   What materials are needed to build a bridge? Where would you get these materials? Give the steps, in order, for building a bridge.

4.   Draw a "pretend" bridge. Make it unusual, one that everyone would want to come and see. What would you name your bridge?

5.   Who could you have sent over the bridge to deal with the troll?

Communication

    1.   List words or draw pictures that describe the three Billy Goats, the troll, the bridge, and the pasture.

    2.   How did the little Billy Goat feel when he heard the mean old troll say, "Who is crossing over my bridge?" How did the troll feel when the biggest Billy Goat challenged him to a fight? Have you ever felt sad, mad, or scared? Draw pictures of these times.

    3.   Was the troll tricked by the Billy Goats Gruff? Did he deserve what happened to him?

Forecasting/Decision-Making

    1.   List as many reasons as you can think of that the old troll did not want them crossing his bridge.

    2.   Why didn't the three Billy Goats Gruff cross the bridge together?

    3.   What do you think happened to the Billy Goats and the troll months later?

    4.   What would have happened if the troll had come up to see the smallest Billy Goat?

    5.   Name three ways the goats could have made their own pasture better for eating.

    6.   Name two things the goats and the troll could have said or done to have made their "community" a better place in which to live peacefully.

Follow-Through Activities

    •   Make a family tree through four generations of your family (parents, grandparents, great-grandparents, great-great-grandparents). Talk to someone in your family (parents or grandparents, for example) about this project.

    •   Paint a picture of a place near your house where the goats could live.

THE THREE BILLY GOATS GRUFF

Circle the object in each row that is different.

Productive Thinking

1.   List the materials needed to build the pigs' houses. What would be the good and bad features of each kind of material?

2.   List as many materials as you can that could be used to make homes.

3.   If this were a real story, how would the wolf get into the pigpen?

4.   Home is a place where you feel comfortable, safe, and secure. Name some forest animals and describe their homes.

5.   List other farm animals and the names of their babies.

6.   Build homes similar to the three little pigs' homes (sugar cubes can simulate brick).

Planning

1.   What factors could determine a person's choice of a home? (Consider materials available, cost, climate, size of the family, etc.)

2.   Identify or draw the steps the pigs would take to build their houses.

3.   Draw a map showing the three little pigs' homes, wolf's woods, fair, apple tree, etc.

4.   The pigs ran very fast to their brother's house made of bricks. Estimate how long it would take you to get from school to home by walking, riding in a car, or riding your bike.

5.   Mother Pig had three little pigs in her family. Write a story about your family.

Communication

1. Why do you think Mother Pig sent the little pigs out into the world?

2. Mother Pig sent the three little pigs out into the world with the same amount of money for each. Did each pig spend his money wisely? Explain your answer.

3. Make up a story in which the pigs use their money in a way other than buying building materials.

4. How do you think the third little pig felt when he heard the wolf on the roof? What were his thoughts?

5. Would you rather be a pig or the wolf in the story? Why?

6. Describe your favorite room in your house, apartment, etc.

Forecasting/Decision-Making

1. Suppose the wolf asked in a gentle voice, "Little pig, little pig, please let me come in." What would have happened if the pigs had let him in?

2. The wolf blew the straw and stick houses down. What other ways could he have gotten in with the pigs?

3. If the main character were a man instead of a wolf, how would the story change?

4. Make up a new ending to the story, beginning with the wolf on the roof and the pigs inside the brick house.

5. If you were the first little pig and your house was blown down, would you hide in the straw, fight, or run to safety? Tell why.

6. If you were the wolf, how would you get the pigs to come out of their homes?

7. Do you think the three little pigs can all live together happily? What problems might they have?

Follow-Through Activities

• Make up a play using a modern setting. A robber enters a house in the neighborhood. The neighbor runs out the back door. Finish the play. Maybe you would like to produce it.

THE THREE LITTLE PIGS

Home is a place where you feel safe and secure.
Draw lines to match these animals with their homes.

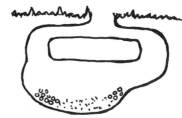

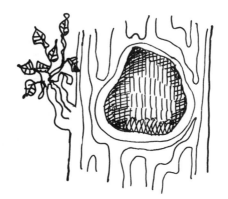

© 1992 by Incentive Publications, Inc., Nashville, TN.

THE THREE LITTLE PIGS

Pretend your mother has given you $5.00 to spend on whatever you like.

Circle the things you will buy with your money.

2.00

CANDY BAR

.50

3.00

3.00

4.00

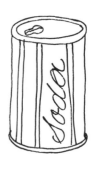

.50

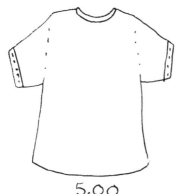

5.00

1.00

2.00

© 1992 by Incentive Publications, Inc., Nashville, TN.

THE THREE WISHES

Productive Thinking

1. Why was the woodcutter poor?

2. What else could the woodsman sell from the forest besides firewood?

3. Draw a picture of what you think a tree fairy looks like.

4. Do you think the woodsman meant to use one of his wishes on sausage?

5. What parts of this story could actually be real, and what parts have to be pretend?

Planning

1. The woodcutter and his wife thought of many things to wish for. Which of their ideas were the wisest?

2. How could they have covered the sausage or gotten rid of it without spending a wish?

3. Was the woodcutter a good husband? Was the woodcutter's wife a good wife? Explain your answer.

Communication

1. The woodsman always dreamed that he would be rich and have a big house and plenty of food. Have you ever had a dream? Tell about it.

2. If the tree fairy gave you a wish, what would you wish?

3. Evaluate the wife's behavior throughout the story (when she heard about the tree fairy, when she was thinking of wishes, when she scolded her husband, when she had the sausage nose, when they had used their wishes).

Forecasting/Decision-Making

1. The woodcutter said he could get used to the sausage on his wife's nose. Suppose he did. Make up a new ending.

2. Retell the story with the woodcutter and his wife agreeing on the three wishes that would make them happy.

3. What would happen if the woodcutter went back to the tree fairy? Finish the story.

4. How is this story like "The Magic Fish" or "The Magic Tablecloth?" How are these stories different?

Follow-Through Activities

• Make a fishing game using a magnet on the end of a string and paper clips glued to paper fish. Catch the fish.

• Draw or make a list of your favorite things: food, hobby, friends, television program, summer fun, clothing, favorite day of the week, etc.

Answers for puzzle on page 99:
Wet Weather: cloud, flood, rainy, storm, soggy, drops, water
Sunny Weather: beams, warm, light, shine, clear, fresh, dries, sunny

---

THE THREE WISHES

Many times when it rains we wish for sunshine.
Unscramble these weather words.
Write the unscrambled words on the lines below.

WET WEATHER WORDS

UCDOL

_____

GSYOG

_____

OFDLO

_____

RSOMT

_____

SPORD

_____

YANRI

_____

RTEWA

_____

SUNNY DAY WORDS

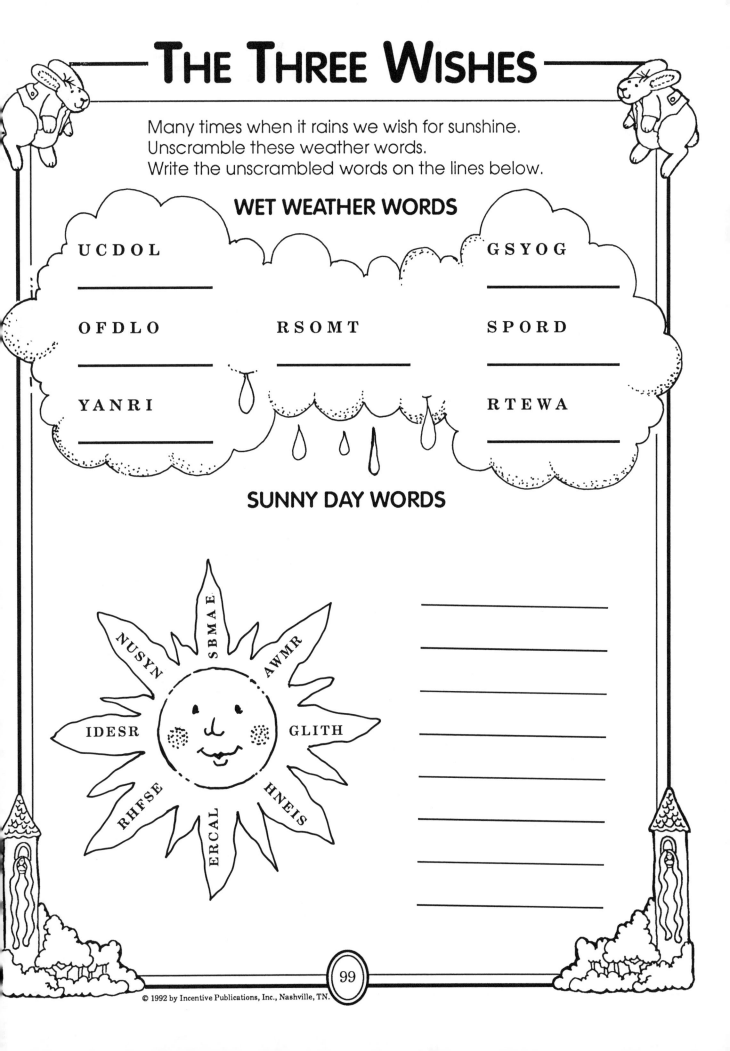

SBMAE

NUSYN

AWMR

IDESR

GLITH

RHFSE

ERCAL

HNEIS

_____

_____

_____

_____

_____

_____

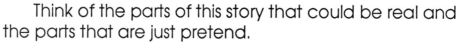
THE THREE WISHES

Think of the parts of this story that could be real and the parts that are just pretend.
Write **real** or **pretend** under each picture.

_____

_____

_____

_____

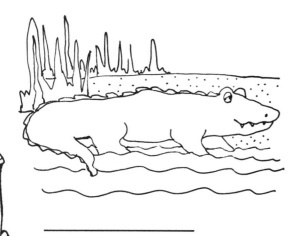

_____

_____

THUMBELINA

Productive Thinking

1. The woman wanted a child. She went to the witch for advice. Who else could she have asked for advice?

2. This seed grew into a flower and bloomed in one night. How long does it usually take a tulip to grow? Draw its life cycle.

3. What dangers would Thumbelina have because she was so tiny?

4. How did Thumbelina get to be queen of the flowers?

5. Why did Thumbelina need wings?

Planning

1. Thumbelina was the size of your thumb. What would she use for a cradle, a dish, etc.?

2. Make up a song Thumbelina might sing.

3. When Thumbelina awakened, she found herself trapped on a lily pad. How could she be freed? Change the story.

4. What do you think the little old woman did when she saw Thumbelina was gone?

Communication

1. Why do you think Father Toad thought Thumbelina would make a good wife for his son?

2. Why didn't the beetle think Thumbelina was pretty?

3. What did Thumbelina do that made the mole fall in love with her?

4. Why didn't Thumbelina leave with the swallow the first time? Have you ever wanted to do something but you just couldn't?

5. What made the mouse think the mole would be a good husband? Why did Thumbelina think differently?

Forecasting/Decision-Making

1.   Do you think the woman thought if she planted the barley corn she would get a child?

2.   What would have happened if Thumbelina had awakened as the frog carried her to the river? Finish the story.

3.   How could Thumbelina and the mole have adjusted their life together to be happy?

4.   Compare the stories of "Thumbelina" and "Tom Thumb". How are they alike? How are they different?

Follow-Through Activities

•   Draw or name places Thumbelina could go that you can't because of your size.

•   Make flowers from construction paper. Maybe Thumbelina would like to live in one of them.

•   Make a finger puppet of Thumbelina. Tell the story in the first person ("I").

•   Debate whether it is better to be small or large in stature.

Thumbelina

Thumbelina loved sunshine; the mole loved darkness. These are opposite. Go on a word hunt. Every word listed below has an opposite word in the puzzle. Look up, down, forward and backward, and circle as many as you can find. Mark out each word on the list as you find its opposite, and write the opposite beside it.

```
                  D
           H  A  D
       D   O  Y  O  B
   M   A  N  S  W  A  L
F  A  R  O  U  N  D  I  E
D  K  S  M  I  L  E
   C  O  M  E  S
   W  E  T
      R
```

WORD LIST

_____ daughter	_____ good	_____ saner
_____ don't	_____ hadn't	_____ square
_____ dry	_____ light	_____ truth
_____ frown	_____ live	_____ up
_____ girl	_____ near	_____ winter
_____ goes	_____ night	_____ woman

Productive Thinking

1.   Think of many different and unusual animals who could have raced against each other. Who would have won? Why?

2.   Draw your favorite forest animals in the race.

3.   Draw the body parts of various animals that would help make them sure winners.

4.   Make a list of other ways to get the news of the Big Race to all the animals.

5.   When the turtle passed the rabbit, the rabbit was sleeping. Draw or list what you think the rabbit was dreaming about.

6.   Make banners that would make the animals interested in attending the race.

7.   Make up math problems, calculating who would win and how long it would take.

Planning

1.   The rabbit and the turtle ran the race from the big rock to the tree. Make an obstacle course that would be more interesting than this empty roadway.

2.   The animals stood around waiting for the race to begin. What other activities could they have thought of to make the day more fun?

3.   Choose two different animals. Write the rules for their race. Make sure it is fair for both animals.

4.   The fox said, "One, two, three, go!" to start the race. If the animals were making so much noise that the turtle and the hare could not hear, what would you do?

5.   Plan a sack race. Tell the steps in order from planning the activity to announcing the winner. List materials needed. What would be a good prize?

6.   What problems might develop before the race? During the race? How would you solve these problems?

7.   If the turtle accidentally turned over on his back during the race, what would you as the referee do?

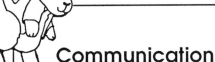

Communication

1. List some characteristics that helped the turtle win. Name some reasons the hare lost.

2. Pair some animals together that would make an interesting, fair race. (Animals with like abilities.)

3. Why did the turtle challenge the hare to the race? What other animal would have been a better match for the turtle? Why? What other animal would have been a better match for the rabbit? Why?

4. How do you think the turtle felt before the race? Did the animals laughing at him make him feel more confident? Think of as many comparisons as you can to describe the turtle's sadness. The turtle was as sad as . . .

5. Sometimes it is hard to tell others how you feel. Draw pictures to show how you think these two animals felt before and after the race.

6. The rabbit kept boasting that he was the fastest animal in the forest. List the reasons he might have felt this way.

Forecasting/Decision-Making

1. It was a beautiful day for the race. What if hunters were seen in the woods that day? List changes in the plans for the race. How would you tell everyone about the changes?

2. What would be a good prize for the animal that won the race?

3. Will there be another race? What will happen the next time the rabbit and the turtle race?

4. Would you have small neighborhood races or one big race for all the animals? Explain your answer. Discuss the problems of each option.

Follow-Through Activity

• Hold a race between the turtle and the hare. Cut the turtle and hare out of cardboard. Cut two 4-foot lengths of string. Tie each string to the leg of a chair (use one chair). Pass the free end of each string through a hole cut in one of the cardboard animal's heads. Players hold the strings, jerking them up and down to make the animals run.

THE TURTLE AND THE HARE

Choose two different animals to run a race.
Write the rules for the race.
Make sure the race is fair to both animals.

RULES

_____
_____
_____
_____
_____
_____
_____
_____
_____
_____
_____

THE UGLY DUCKLING

Productive Thinking

1.   Name as many animals and their babies as you can. Example: cow – calf.

2.   Some eggs take longer to hatch than others. Do you think it is because they are different sizes, or because they are different kinds of eggs?

3.   Name animals that hatch from eggs.

4.   Compare ducks to swans. How are they alike? How are they different?

5.   The caterpillar can seem very ugly to us—but what does it become?

Planning

1.   It doesn't matter how hot, cold, or rainy the weather, Mother Duck must sit on her eggs. What can she or the drake do to make her waiting time more pleasant?

2.   Mother Duck watched to see if this last little duck acted like a duck. What did he do that ducks do?

3.   As long as the Ugly Duckling tried to be someone he wasn't (duck, cat, rooster), he was very sad. When did his attitude change?

4.   Geese usually migrate south to warmer weather. The Ugly Duckling did not know this. How do you think he survived that first winter?

5.   Talk about the life cycle of a duck. Is a swan's life cycle the same?

6.   Mother Duck was very concerned that one of the eggs would not hatch. If you were Mother Duck, would you continue to sit on the egg or go with the other little ducklings?

Communication

1.   What makes something seem ugly or beautiful to you?

2.   How did the duckling feel when Mother said he was ugly and the other ducks did not want him around? Has anyone ever said something to you that hurt your feelings? What did you do?

3.   The duckling bowed his head toward the water to show he was sad and embarrassed. What body language do we use to show we are sad, mad, happy, frightened, or tired?

4.   Do you think the Ugly Duckling had a good mother?

5.   Which character in this story would you prefer to be?

Forecasting/Decision-Making

1.   How would the story have changed if the Ugly Duckling egg had been in a swan's nest?

2.   If the ducks had been kind to the Ugly Duckling, do you think he would have left the duck pond?

3.   Tell us another adventure about the Ugly Duckling and his new swan friends. Will he go back to the duck pond?

4.   Do you think the Ugly Duckling will be a good father? Why?

Follow-Through Activities

•   Make an ugly face using a paper plate and scrap materials.

•   Use your body to show the various moods and feelings of the characters.

•   Pantomime with a friend. (Examples: playing tennis, robin and a worm, riding on a seesaw.)

THE UGLY DUCKLING

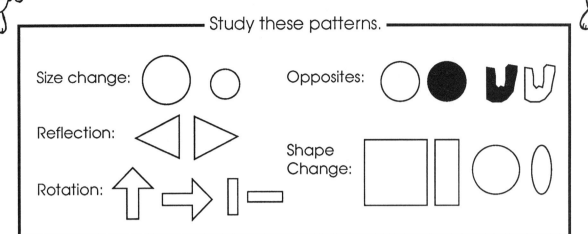

Size change:

Reflection:

Rotation:

Opposites:

Shape Change:

Use the patterns on the left as examples to complete the patterns on the right.

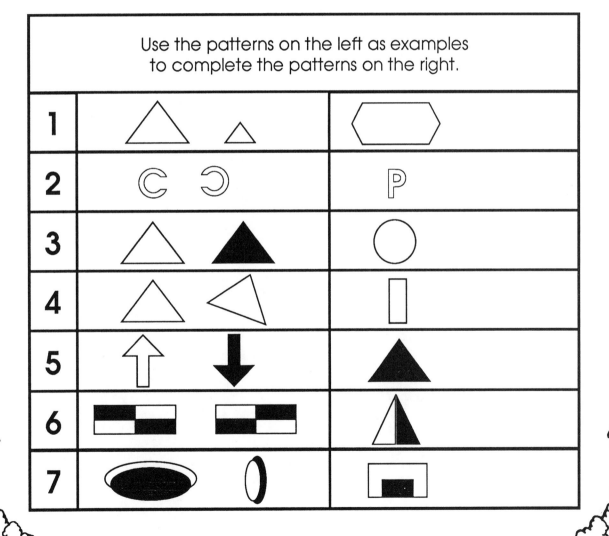

1		
2		
3		
4		
5		
6		
7		

STORIES

ALEXANDER AND THE TERRIBLE, HORRIBLE, NO GOOD, VERY BAD DAY

Productive Thinking

1. What started Alex's day off badly?

2. Alex and his brothers ate cereal for breakfast. Name as many breakfast foods as you can.

3. Why do you think Mrs. Dickens chose Paul's picture of the sailboat instead of Alex's invisible castle?

4. Why did Alex keep thinking about Australia? Had he ever been there?

Planning

1. What could Alex have done that might have made his day better?

2. How could Alex have turned his day around at lunch time?

3. If you were Alex's friend, how would you help him turn his day around?

4. If Alex did not want the white sneakers, what could he have done?

Communication

1. How do you feel when you find a prize in your cereal?

2. Alex was mad at Paul because he wasn't his best friend anymore. He said some things that just made matters worse. What were they? Have you ever said something when you were mad and later were sorry you said it?

3. Would you want Alex for a friend today?

4. Have you ever had a terrible, horrible, bad day? Tell about it. Was it as terrible as Alex's?

Forecasting/Decision-Making

1. Why do you think no one paid any attention to Alex when he said, "If I don't get by a window, I'll get car sick"?

2. Can you think of anything else bad that could have happened to Alex that day?

3. Make up another day for Alex with some good, exciting happenings.

4. If Alex had put away his skateboard and put his chewing gum in the trash can the night before, would his day have started better?

5. What could you do to make Alex's day better?

Follow-Through Activities

- Draw or describe the worst day you have ever had. Show how you felt.

- Interview Alexander for your newspaper.

ALL ABOUT COPY KITTEN

Productive Thinking

1. What other animals did Copy Kitten try to be like?

2. When did he copy them?

3. Why wasn't he successful copying them?

4. Name some furry animals and tell what they do.

5. Name some animals with feathers and tell what they can do.

Planning

1. Why did all the animals like Copy Kitten better at the end of the story?

2. Make a list or draw pictures of what Copy Kitten could have done if he had copied his mother.

3. Copy Kitten thought that whenever animals do the same thing, they are copying. List animals that swim, fly, hop, and jump.

4. Differentiate between the dog's digging and the farmer's digging, the duck's swimming and the fish's swimming.

Communication

1. What made Copy Kitten change his mind about trying to be like the other animals?

2. The poor kitten was sad, disappointed, and, finally, happy. Describe these feelings.

3. How do you think the animals felt when the kitten tried to copy them?

4. Have you ever tried to be like someone else and you just couldn't? Tell about it.

Forecasting/Decision-Making

1.   Which animal was the easiest for Copy Kitten to be like? Explain your answer.

2.   Which animal would be the hardest for Copy Kitten to copy? Why?

3.   Suppose Copy Kitten tried to copy a horse or a snake. Make up a story about this.

4.   Discuss how life would have been different for Copy Kitten had he followed his mother.

5.   Interpret or explain the thought: "It is better just to be yourself."

Follow-Through Activities

•   Leader performs an action such as wiggling nose, clapping hands, touching ear, etc. Other children must copy the action when signaled to do so. Several actions can be used if the children have good memory recall.

•   Copy a design on the blackboard. Cover it. See if the children can draw it from memory.

AMELIA BEDELIA

Productive Thinking

1. What was Amelia's job and who did she work for?

2. Amelia had problems with Mrs. Rogers's directions to dust the furniture, draw the drapes when the sun came in, and dress the chicken for dinner. What did Amelia do?

3. Draw a picture of the Rogers's home from information you got from the story.

4. Write Amelia Bedelia's resumé, listing her skills.

Planning

1. Name some jobs in your house Amelia could do. Give her directions very carefully.

2. Create a new adventure for Amelia.

3. Compare Amelia's and Mrs. Rogers's attitudes.

4. Read a recipe and tell how Amelia would interpret it.

Communication

1. If you were Mr. and Mrs. Rogers, how would you feel about Amelia?

2. How did Amelia feel when Mrs. Rogers became angry?

3. What made Mrs. Rogers very angry? What was she ready to do?

4. Would you keep Amelia Bedelia as your housekeeper?

5. Describe feeling happy, feeling sad.

Forecasting/Decision-Making

1. What would have happened if Amelia Bedelia hadn't baked the pie?

2.   Was Amelia a good housekeeper? Explain your answer.

3.   Do you think Amelia and Mr. and Mrs. Rogers can live together happily?

4.   Put Amelia in a computer lab. What would happen? Make up a new story.

5.   Let Amelia work in a flower garden. What would she do there?

Follow-Through Activities

•   Words with more than one meaning confused Amelia. Draw or list as many words with more than one meaning as you can.

•   Fold a paper into quarters. Use a hole punch in the folded paper. Connect the dots to make a picture of the design.

ANGUS AND THE CAT

Productive Thinking

1. Name as many different kinds of dogs as you can.

2. How are Scotty dogs and dachshunds alike? How are they different?

3. As Scottie grew older, he learned many things. Name what he learned.

4. Animals move in many ways. Name some animals and how they move.

5. How are cats and dogs the same? How are they different?

Planning

1. Angus wanted to get to the cat, but his leash was too short. What would you have done if you were Angus?

2. List the adventure Angus had when he found the cat indoors the first three days. What did he like to do?

3. Name some places the cat could hide where Angus could not find her.

4. Make a picture or diorama of where Angus and the cat played indoors. Use the story for reference.

Communication

1. Now that you are older, what have you learned to do and not do?

2. Describe the relationship Angus had with the cat.

3. Why was Angus sad when he couldn't find the cat?

4. How did Angus show the cat he was glad she was back?

Forecasting/Decision-Making

1. What would have happened if Angus had caught the cat?

2. Do you think Angus and the cat will still chase each other, or do you think they will be friends now? Explain your answer.

3. Create a new story with Angus and a balloon.

4. Tell the story from Angus's master's point-of-view.

Follow-Through Activities

•   Angus loves to tease the cat. Draw or tell how you like to tease someone, or draw or tell about someone who likes to tease you.

•   Debate the truth of the following statement: If someone teases you, it means that he or she likes you.

Babar Loses His Crown

Productive Thinking

1. The Babar family packed their bags to go to Paris. What do you think they took in their suitcases?

2. The Babar family rode a train to Paris. What other way might they have gotten there?

3. The porter carried the bags to the hotel room. Name other workers at the hotel.

4. What other instruments besides the flute could have been heard in the orchestra at the opera?

Planning

1. List the steps they took to find the red bag.

2. Name all the ways the Babar family traveled through Paris.

3. Who else besides his family could Babar have gotten to help him find his red bag?

4. What enjoyable things did you see in this book that make you think you would like Paris?

Communication

1. Why do you think Celeste and Babar took their crowns?

2. How did Babar feel when Celeste opened the red bag and there was a flute?

3. Whose fault was it that the bags got mixed up? Explain your answer.

4. Give several reasons the night at the opera was considered a great night for Babar and the mustache man.

Forecasting/Decision-Making

1.   Babar knew they would love Paris. What if they hadn't liked it? Make up a story about this possibility.

2.   Did Babar and his family enjoy Paris? Explain your answer.

3.   Would the family have enjoyed Paris more if they hadn't lost the red bag? Create a story about this.

4.   Suppose Babar had never found his crown. Would he still be king? What would he have done? Finish the story.

Follow-Through Activities

•   Use construction paper and bangles, etc., to make a crown Babar would love.

•   Use sponges, spools, lids, etc., for print art.

CURIOUS GEORGE

Productive Thinking

1. How did the man catch George? Can you think of another way he could have caught him?

2. On the ship, George tried to fly like the seagulls. Why couldn't he fly?

3. Name three times George's curiosity got him into trouble.

4. How did the fireman know where the call was coming from? What do firemen do to prepare for a fire?

5. If you were a zookeeper, what animals would you want in your zoo? Where would you get them?

Planning

1. What are some activities George and the man could have done on the big ship?

2. What would have happened to George if he had not escaped from prison? Make up a story about this.

3. If you were given the responsibility of taking care of George, what would you do? How can you be sure George will have a safe trip to the states?

4. What would have happened if George had let go of the balloon?

5. The man in the big yellow hat paid for all the balloons. How much do you think this probably cost him?

Communication

1. Why were the firemen so mad when they found out George was playing with the phone?

2. How did George feel when the wind whisked him and the balloons away? What did the people below think?

3. How did George and the man in the yellow hat get along? Did they have a good relationship?

4. Has being curious ever gotten you into trouble at home or at school? Tell about it.

Forecasting/Decision-Making

1. George escaped prison by walking the telephone wires. If George had been a rabbit, would the story have changed? Write or tell about it.

2. Will George adjust to being in a zoo? What adventures might he have there?

3. Would George have a better life in the jungles of Africa or in the zoo here in America? Explain your answer.

4. What if George had been found by a little boy in the country? How would the story change? What would happen to George?

5. Decide if George would be happiest in a zoo or a circus.

6. Do you think George is smart? Explain why.

Follow-Through Activity

- If George had been in charge of the zoo, he would have changed it. Write or draw pictures of reasons you think he would or would not make a good zookeeper.

FLIP AND THE COWS

Productive Thinking

1.   Why do you think Flip was afraid of the cows?

2.   Compare a cow and a horse. How are they alike? How are they different?

3.   Why do some cows have horns?

4.   What else might Flip have seen in the pasture?

5.   Name some baby farm animals and their parents.

6.   Draw a farm scene including Flip.

Planning

1.   Would jumping across the brook backward be the same as jumping forward?

2.   What other tricks might Flip enjoy practicing in the pasture?

3.   What caused Flip's accident with Mother?

4.   Flip's plan was to back up and jump over the cows. Why didn't the plan work?

5.   If Flip grows up to be a cowboy's horse, will cows be afraid of him?

Communication

1.   Flip did not know why he was afraid of cows. Was there ever a time when you felt afraid and did not know why? Tell about that time.

2.   Flip felt secure with the fence between him and the cows. Was he safe?

3.   How did Flip act when he was scared? What happens to you when *you* are scared?

4. What did Flip do when his mother nipped him?

5. What made Flip go beserk— jumping high, turning somersaults, etc. ?

Forecasting/Decision-Making

1. Flip heard the cows mooing. He could not run; he was out of breath. What would have happened if Flip had talked back to the cows by neighing?

2. If Flip hadn't bumped into a cow's horn, do you think he would still be afraid of cows?

3. Pretend you are Flip. Tell Mother about your adventure with the cows.

4. If there had been a calf in the field, would Flip have been afraid then?

5. Predict what will happen the next time Flip finds himself in the cow's pasture.

Follow-Through Activities

• Make a Flip with dough (2 parts flour, 1 part salt, $\frac{1}{4}$ part water).

Productive Thinking

1.   Why did Toad make a list of the day's activities?

2.   Why would Toad help Frog catch the list?

3.   What really made Toad's garden grow?

4.   When it came to eating cookies, did Frog and Toad have willpower?

5.   Were Toad and Frog brave? List the reasons for your answer.

Planning

1.   Make a list of your day's activities. Follow it as closely as Toad did.

2.   What did Toad do to try to make his garden grow?

3.   List the ways in which Toad and Frog tried to keep from eating the cookies.

4.   What else could Toad and Frog do about their cookie problem?

5.   Which of Frog and Toad's adventures do you think was most dangerous? Do you think they reacted to the situations well?

Communication

1.   List some things Frog did that made Toad know he was a good friend.

2.   How did Toad and Frog feel when the little plants came up?

3.   Why do you think Frog gave the cookies to the birds?

4.   What actions showed Frog and Toad were afraid?

5.   Do you think Toad wished his dream were true? Why?

Forecasting/Decision-Making

1.   Did Toad control his own actions? Explain your answer.

2.   What do you think will happen when Toad gets the cake baked? Write a story about it.

3.   After Frog and Toad came out of their closets, what new adventures do you think they had? Make up a story about a new adventure.

4.   Assume Toad's dream had been true. What would happen then?

Follow-Through Activities

•   Design a raft on which Frog and Toad could ride together. Use craft sticks.

•   Frog and Toad were very different, but they had a good friendship. Make up a story about your friendship with a visitor from Mars.

GILBERTO AND THE WIND

Productive Thinking

1. What different sounds does the wind make?

2. If the wind gets too strong it becomes a storm. Name different kinds of storms.

3. List reasons Gilberto was angry with the wind.

4. Name some "good deeds" the wind did.

Planning

1. Why did Gilberto think it would be fun to play in the whispering wind with his balloon?

2. Create a new story about Gilberto and the ocean.

3. How can we use the wind to help us?

4. What do you do if the wind is too strong? If you know a hurricane or tornado is coming? How can you be safe?

Communication

1. The wind blew the big boys' kites, but it wouldn't blow Gilberto's. Is this true? Why wouldn't Gilberto's kite fly?

2. How did Gilberto feel when the wind tried to get into his house?

3. Contrast Gilberto's feelings about the wind at different times.

4. What is the difference between a breeze and a storm? How are they alike?

Forecasting/Decision-Making

1.   Gilberto ran through the grass while the wind ran over the top of the grass. Would Gilberto have won the race if the grass had been short? Explain your answer.

2.   Make a model of a windmill. Tell how it can be useful.

3.   Is the wind useful or harmful? Explain your answer.

4.   Make up a new story told from the wind's point of view. Tell how the wind wanted to play with Gilberto.

Follow-Through Activities

•   Make wind toys, cutting and folding paper to make pinwheels, paper helicopters, and paper airplanes.

•   Have a wind race. Choose different objects and see how much time it takes you to blow each one off the table.

HARRY, THE DIRTY DOG

Productive Thinking

1. Harry liked everything except taking a bath. Name some things he liked.

2. When Harry heard the water running in the bathtub, he knew what was coming next. What was it?

3. Harry buried the scrubbing brush in the backyard. Where else could he have hidden it?

4. Draw a map of Harry's adventure.

Planning

1. Harry ran away from home when he didn't want a bath. What would have been a better way to handle the problem?

2. What did Harry do to help the family know who he was?

3. After a bath and a good dinner, Harry dreamed of getting dirty. Make up a new story of another "dirty" adventure.

4. Design a jacket for Harry that will keep him from getting so dirty.

5. Compare Harry's attitudes towards baths at the beginning and end of this story.

Communication

1. Why do you think Harry did not like a bath?

2. Is there anything you don't like to do but have to do? Tell about it.

3. Why did Harry suddenly wish he were home?

4. Tell us Harry's feelings when:

   . . . he played tag with other dogs.

   . . . he wanted to go home.

   . . . the family did not understand him.

   . . . the children cleaned him up.

Forecasting/Decision-Making

1.	No one recognized Harry; he was a black dog. Suppose they locked him outside the fence. What could Harry have done?

2.	What if Harry didn't find his scrubbing brush? Would the family know what Harry wanted?

3.	How can Harry show the family he wants something to eat, wants to go outside, or wants to play?

4.	Is this a real or pretend story?

Follow-Through Activities

•	Draw or describe what Harry looked like when he was dirty and when he was clean.

•	Name or draw some activities that "require" getting dirty.

IRA SLEEPS OVER

Productive Thinking

1. Ira was invited over to his friend Reggie's house to spend the night. What will he need to take with him?

2. Did Ira think he could sleep without his teddy bear?

3. Reggie had many fun things planned for them to do at his house. Name them.

4. Reggie had a junk collection. What kind of junk might a 6- or 7-year-old boy collect?

5. What made Ira decide to go back home and get his teddy bear Tah-tah?

Planning

1. Why was Ira afraid to take his teddy bear to Reggie's house?

2. Plan your best friend's visit to your house. What will you do for fun?

3. Ira and Reggie lay in the bed telling scary stories. Make up a ghost story that might scare the boys.

Communication

1. When you were young, did you have a favorite stuffed animal? Tell about it. Did it have a special name?

2. Why did Reggie and Ira want their teddy bears?

3. Ira was afraid to take Tah-tah with him for fear he would be laughed at. Have you ever been afraid your peers would laugh at you? Tell about it.

4. Do you have a collection which you show to your friends? What kind of collection do you have, and where do you keep it?

5. How would a sleep-over at Grandma's be different from a sleep-over at a friend's? How would they be the same?

Forecasting/Decision-Making

1.   Would there have been anything questionable about Ira taking his toy cars or his army men to Reggie's? Why or why not?

2.   Suppose Reggie loaned Ira one of his bears to sleep with. Would this be the same as having his own bear with him?

3.   When Reggie and Ira wake up in the morning, will they talk about their bears Tah-tah and Too-foo? Make up a story about the next morning.

4.   When Reggie goes to stay all night with Ira, what do you think he will take with him?

Follow-Through Activities

•   Draw or color a picture of Ira and Reggie. Now make it a nighttime picture by covering it with thin, black tempera paint.

KATY NO-POCKET

Productive Thinking

1. Katy was very sad because she did not have a pocket. Why did she need and want a pocket?

2. Tell us the problem from the baby kangaroo Freddy's point of view.

3. List or draw various ways animals carry their babies.

4. The wise owl told Katy to get a pocket. Name some people who need aprons with pockets when they work.

5. Katy got a carpenter's apron. What did the carpenter carry in his pockets?

Planning

1. Katy could not carry Freddy on her head as the crocodile did because Freddy could not hang on. What could Katy have done to keep him from falling off?

2. Katy could not carry her baby in her arms because her arms weren't long enough. Do you have any idea how Katy could carry her baby?

3. What are some other problems Katy might have had with Freddy?

4. Why was Katy able to hop home faster than she could hop to the city?

5. What would Katy have done if some of the animals had been too big for her pockets?

Communication

1. How did the animals show that they felt sorry for Katy and understood her problem?

2. Why did Katy fill up all the pockets with baby animals? How did this make her feel?

3. At the beginning of the story, Katy was very sad and troubled. At the end Katy was happy and satisfied. What made the difference in her attitude?

4. Katy did not know they sold pockets in the city. How did she feel when she got to the town? How did she know where to go?

5. Do you know any other stories where the animals ask the "Wise Ole Owl" for advice?

Forecasting/Decision-Making

1. Judge whether or not Katy was a good parent. Explain.

2. Make up a story about a young deer looking for antlers.

3. Katy shared her pockets with the other animals. What could they share with her? What relationships among the animals would help make a nice community?

4. Katy can no longer be called Katy No-Pocket. Think of a new name for her.

5. Is this a real or pretend story? Explain your answer.

Follow-Through Activities

•   Name or draw the animals that you think would fit into Katy's pockets.

•   Role-play this story.

Lovable Lyle

Productive Thinking

1.   How did the bakery lady, ice cream man, the bird, and the children show Lyle they loved him?

2.   What did Lyle do to make himself so lovable?

3.   Analyze Mrs. Primm's words: "It isn't always possible to please everyone or be liked by everyone, no matter how we try."

4.   Why didn't Clover like Lyle? Why couldn't they be friends?

5.   At the end of the story, why did Clover send Lyle a love note?

Planning

1.   How do you think Lyle could have found his enemy?

2.   What did Lyle do to show everyone he was nice? Can you think of anything else he could have done to get people to like him?

3.   Describe the Primms's plan to get Clover's mother to meet Lyle. Why didn't it work?

4.   Draw pictures of Lyle's water stunts.

5.   What are the activities in this story that make it a pretend story?

Communication

1.   Would you have loved Lyle? Explain your answer.

2.   How did Lyle feel when he found out he had an enemy? Has anyone ever told you he or she did not like you? How did you feel?

3.   Describe the relationship between the Primm family and Lyle.

4. When Lyle was to meet Clover's mother, he got a negative thought (maybe she won't like me) and became shy. Has this ever happened to you?

5. Lyle rescued Clover, who was drowning. How did he feel about himself now?

Forecasting/Decision-Making

1. If Lyle were a dog, would the story be different? Make up this story.

2. Tell the story from Lyle's point of view.

3. Why did the author choose to make Lyle, the main character, a crocodile instead of a dog or cat?

4. If Lyle had met Clover's mother with his best manners, would the story be different? Finish it.

Follow-Through Activities

• Lovable Lyle's name begins with the letter "L." Make some silly sentences using the same initial consonants as a person's name. Example: Lovable Lyle likes to lick lollipops.

• Make a shadow puppet of Lyle.

• Make a mobile of scary animals: Bend a coat hanger into a circular shape; string animals on it.

• Make a scary puppet from a small brown sack and construction paper.

MAKE WAY FOR DUCKLINGS

Productive Thinking

1. Mr. and Mrs. Mallard were having a hard time finding a good place to raise their ducklings. Analyze the ducks' needs.

2. Make a model of the little island in Charles River that Mrs. Mallard liked so much.

3. How long does it take for duck eggs to hatch?

4. The Mallards gave their eight ducklings rhyming names. Can you think of some other rhyming names for the next family of ducklings?

Planning

1. Why couldn't the ducks stay in the park all day? Why was it dangerous?

2. If you were the park ranger, how would you take care of Mr. and Mrs. Mallard and the ducklings?

3. How did Michael and the other policemen save the ducks' lives?

4. Tell about a day in the life of Mr. and Mrs. Mallard.

Communication

1. How did Michael, the policeman, and the ducks become friends?

2. How did Mr. and Mrs. Mallard feel about their eight little ducklings? How did Mrs. Mallard show her feelings?

3. Describe what happened at the traffic jam. Everyone was angry. Why?

4. Mr. Mallard found a waterway to their island nest. Is this a better way than Mom's route?

Forecasting/Decision-Making

1.   What did Mother Mallard have to teach her ducklings?

2.   Why did the Mallards follow the Big Seven boat? What will happen in the winter when the Big Seven boat won't travel up the river?

3.   How did Mr. and Mrs. Mallard spend the winters? Make up an adventure about this.

4.   Were Mr. and Mrs. Mallard good parents?

5.   Make a map showing the two routes from the island to the park (one by water, the other by boat).

Follow-Through Activities

•   Draw or paint a picture of the park. Be sure to add Mrs. Mallard and her ducklings.

•   Waddle across the room like a duck.

•   Name or draw mother animals and their babies. Draw as many as you can.

Productive Thinking

1.   What did Grandma send Harry for his birthday?

2.   Name the places Harry tried to lose the sweater. Why didn't he succeed?

3.   A bird picked up a thread from Harry's sweater and unraveled the whole sweater. What was the bird going to do with the wool?

4.   Tell the story from Harry's point of view.

Planning

1.   Harry did not like the roses on his sweater. Design one you think he would like.

2.   If Harry were your dog, what would you do?

3.   Name a variety of materials that could have been used for Harry's coat.

4.   Using information given in the story, draw a map of Harry's neighborhood.

Communication

1.   How did Harry feel when he wore the rose sweater downtown?

2.   Have you ever received a gift you didn't like? What did you do?

3.   Why do you think Harry didn't tell the children about the sweater?

4.   How do you think Harry felt when he got the rose sweater, when the bird took it, when he heard Grandma was coming, and when he showed Grandma the nest?

Forecasting/Decision-Making

1.   If Harry had been a cat, would the story have changed?

2.   What do you think Grandma will send Harry next Christmas?

3.   Make up a new adventure about Harry.

4.   How do you think Grandmother felt about the sweater?

Follow-Through Activities

•   Draw or describe something you received as a gift that you did not like.

•   Design a sweater you think Harry would like.

A POCKET FOR CORDUROY

Productive Thinking

1. Why did Lisa set her bear in the chair?

2. How could Lisa help her mother?

3. Why did Corduroy want a pocket? Why are pockets useful?

4. Why do you think a towel or washcloth could not be used for a pocket?

5. Compare the large laundry bag to Corduroy's natural home, a cave.

6. The laundry bag belonged to an artist. What might he have in his bag to wash?

7. Describe the pocket Lisa made for Corduroy's overalls.

Planning

1. Lisa went to the laundromat with her mother. She had to wait a long time for the laundry to wash and dry. What could Lisa do while she was waiting?

2. What would Corduroy have to do to use the washcloth for a pocket?

3. Why did Corduroy begin playing with the soap flakes?

4. If you were the manager, what would you do with materials left in the laundromat?

5. Draw a picture of the inside of the laundromat.

6. What could Lisa have done if Corduroy had not been in the laundromat?

Communication

1.   How did Lisa feel when she couldn't find Corduroy and the laundromat was closing?

2.   Why did the artist feel he should dry Corduroy's overalls?

3.   How did Corduroy feel watching his pants in the dryer?

4.   Corduroy was having lots of fun with the soap flakes until he slid into a cart. How did he feel then? What did he do?

5.   Why did Lisa call Corduroy a little rascal?

6.   At the end of the story, how did Corduroy show Lisa that he loved his pocket? How do you show your mom and dad you like what they do for you?

Forecasting/Decision-Making

1.   What time of day do you think would be the busiest time at the laundromat? Explain your answer.

2.   What can happen to precious things when they are left in pockets at wash time?

3.   What would have happened if the artist had taken Corduroy home with him? Make up a story about this.

4.   Tell the story from Corduroy's viewpoint.

5.   What parts of this story could be real, and what parts are definitely pretend?

6.   Make up a new story about Corduroy looking for boots in the closet or under the bed.

Follow-Through Activities

•   Draw pictures or make a list of people who would find pockets useful for holding objects for their work or play.

•   Cut strips of paper. Lay them on dark paper to make a design for the pocket.

THE SNEETCHES

Productive Thinking

1. There was only one thing different about all the Sneetches. What was it?

2. Give two reasons Sylvester McMonkey McBean was a good businessman and a good salesman.

3. How did the Sneetches get the stars to stay on?

4. The Sneetches were so busy putting the stars on and taking them off that they couldn't tell who was who. Do you have an idea how to tell the difference between the groups?

Planning

1. We do not see the inside of this peculiar machine that puts stars on their bellies. Draw a picture showing how it probably worked.

2. Draw another picture of the Star-off machine. How is it different?

3. Do you think the beaches will be a better place to live now?

4. How do you select your friends? List your friends and tell why you like them.

Communication

1. How did the Plain-Belly Sneetches feel when they couldn't play ball or go on picnics?

2. How do you think the Sneetches felt going into the machine? How do you think they felt coming out?

3. Have you ever known anyone who was snooty? What made him or her this way? How could you help him or her not to be this way?

4.   Explain this sentence: "They decided Sneetches are Sneetches, and no kind of Sneetch is the best on the beach."

5.   Have you ever not been chosen for a game? How did you feel?

Forecasting/Decision-Making

1.   Why could Sylvester McMonkey McBean raise his price several times?

2.   What would have happened if the Sneetches had run out of money? Finish the story as if this had happened.

3.   Suppose all the brown-eyed children would not play with those who had blue eyes. What would happen? Make up a story about this.

4.   Which is more important, how you look or how you act? Explain your answer.

5.   If Sylvester McMonkey McBean comes back to the beach with his Star-on, Star-off machine, will he have any business? Why?

Follow-Through Activities

•   Peer pressure can be hard to cope with. Name or draw something you have felt you must have so much that you told your parents, "Everyone has it."

•   Think of something you wouldn't dare ask your mom or dad for. Tell why.

THE SNOWY DAY

Productive Thinking

1. Describe what Peter saw as he looked out his window at the white world.

2. List or draw clothing that should be worn outside in the wintertime.

3. Tell how the pathways and roadways were cleared before Peter awakened.

4. What noises do you hear in the snow?

5. What are some winter sports played in the snow?

Planning

1. Name as many ways as you can think of that you could make tracks in the snow. Draw pictures of the tracks.

2. Explain how you make a snow angel in the snow.

3. Make a pretend snowman. Use material you have at home to decorate him or her.

4. Peter put a snowball in his pocket to save until the next day. What do you think happened to it? What would have been a better place to put the snowball?

Communication

1. Peter was having so much fun in the snow. Why did he come in?

2. Pretend you are Peter. Tell your mother about your adventure in the white world.

3. While Peter slept, he dreamed the sun melted all the snow away. Have you ever had a dream you are glad did not come true? Tell about it.

4. What time of the year (summer, spring, fall, or winter) do you like the best? Explain your answer.

Forecasting/Decision-Making

1.   Peter and his friend went out again in the snow. Tell about his second day in the snow.

2.   What would happen if snowflakes were colored? Draw a picture of this.

3.   What would Peter and his friend do if the snow changed to rain?

4.   Make a mural of Peter's adventures in the snow.

Follow-Through Activities

•   Fold a square of white paper in half. Then fold it in thirds, making the folds diagonal and keeping a center point. Cut out differently-shaped pieces and open up for your snowflake.

•   Draw and color a picture. With a toothbrush and white tempera paint, spatter "snow" on your picture.

Productive Thinking

1. What did most of the little bulls like to do? How was Ferdinand different?

2. Ferdinand loved to smell the flowers. Name as many different kinds of flowers as you can.

3. The men who came to choose the bulls for the bullfights wore funny hats. Draw some hats for them.

4. Why did Ferdinand all of a sudden jump, snort, butt, and paw?

5. Describe the gala of the bullfight.

Planning

1. What did the little bulls do to prepare themselves for the bullfights in Madrid?

2. What did the bulls do to seem fierce?

3. Ferdinand was taken to Madrid in a cart. What other ways could he have gotten there?

4. Ferdinand came into the middle of the ring and just sat down. What could the bullfighters do to get him mad?

Communication

1. Ferdinand had a favorite spot he liked. Do you have a special place you like?

2. If you were stung by a bee, how would you act?

3. From the content in the story, would you rather be a Banderillo, Picadore, or the Matador? Why?

4. With Ferdinand's personality, he would have been a better _____ than a bull.

Forecasting/Decision-Making

1.   Do you think Ferdinand's mother was a good mother to just let Ferdinand sit under the trees and smell the flowers? Explain your answer.

2.   If Ferdinand had sat under a tree with no bee, would he have been chosen to go to Madrid? Why or why not?

3.   If Ferdinand had fought the Matador, would the story have been different? Finish the story as if this had happened.

4.   Was Mother happy to see Ferdinand brought back to the ranch?

5.   Is bullfighting a good sport? Explain your answer.

Follow-Through Activities

- Draw the matador. Put him or her in a colorful costume.

- Role-play the bull and the matador, using a red scarf.

THE TALE OF PETER RABBIT

Productive Thinking

1. Why did Peter Rabbit's family choose to live under the roots of a big fir tree?

2. Mother went to do some errands in town. What do you think she did?

3. Peter ate too much. He ate lettuce, beans, and radishes. Name some other vegetables he might have liked to eat.

4. Compare the tools Mr. McGregor was using to try to catch Peter—rake, sieve, and hoe.

Planning

1. How do we choose our homes?

2. Mother Rabbit did not want the children to go near Mr. McGregor's garden because Father had had an accident there. Make up a story about Father Rabbit.

3. Peter slipped under the gate. What other way could he have used to get into the garden?

4. Peter could not find the gate because he was so scared. What should he have done?

5. Mr. McGregor used Peter's jacket and shoes for a scarecrow. How else could he have used them?

6. How would the story change if Mr. McGregor had caught Peter instead of catching just his jacket?

Communication

1.   Why do you think Peter ran straight to Mr. McGregor's garden?

2.   Was Mr. McGregor trying to kill Peter with the rake or just scare him?

3.   Peter was so afraid that he couldn't find the gate. Have you ever been so afraid you couldn't think? Tell about it.

4.   Peter was ready to give up, but his friends the sparrows begged him to try to get loose. Have you ever had a friend that encouraged you to do something? Tell about it.

5.   Why did Mr. McGregor give up trying to catch Peter?

6.   Why didn't Peter want to pick berries like his brothers and sisters?

Forecasting/Decision-Making

1.   Why didn't Peter talk to the white cat? Make an adventure story about this.

2.   Suppose Peter came back looking for his jacket. What would have happened?

3.   What if Peter was a bear instead of a rabbit? Would Mr. McGregor chase him inside a hole? How would the story change?

Follow-Through Activities

•   Prepare something simple like pudding, popcorn, gelatin, or bakeless cookies.

•   Have a tasting party . . . taste something sour, sweet, bitter, and salty.

THE TALE OF PETER RABBIT

Make a map of Peter Rabbit's adventure through Mr. McGregor's garden.

Include lettuce, beans, radishes, tools, and Peter's home under the fir tree.

Draw four different types of homes in which you might live.

THE WIZARD OF OZ

Productive Thinking

1.   A cyclone took Dorothy and Toto into the Land of Oz. Describe a cyclone.

2.   Name as many different kinds of weather storms as you can. Draw pictures or describe the storms.

3.   The Tin Woodsman rusted because he was made of tin and was caught in the rain. Name other things made of tin.

4.   What do we now do to tin to try to keep it from rusting?

5.   Water melted away the Wicked Witch of the West. What do you think she was made of?

Planning

1.   How did Dorothy know how to get to Emerald City?

2.   Along the way Dorothy met a scarecrow, a tin man, and a lion who had problems, too. What were their problems?

3.   Why did the Scarecrow, the Tin Man, and the Lion decide to go with Dorothy?

4.   Make a map showing the way to Emerald City.

5.   Make puppets resembling the Scarecrow and the Tin Man.

6.   The group all had the same task—to get rid of the Wicked Witch of the West. How would you do this?

Communication

1.   The Land of Oz was beautiful. Why didn't Dorothy want to stay there?

2.   The Lion could not be "King of the Beasts" until he changed. What did he know he had to do?

3.   Emerald City was beautiful and magic. Describe it.

4.   The Wizard was a "big head" to Dorothy, a beautiful fairy to the scarecrow, and a terrible beast to the Tin Woodsman. Why do you think he appeared differently to each guest?

Forecasting/Decision-Making

1.   Dorothy was given the silver shoes for killing the Wicked Witch of the North. Suppose Dorothy had refused the shoes, saying, "I did not kill her; the cyclone did it." Would the story have changed? Finish it.

2.   If the Wizard was only a simple man, how could he grant the Scarecrow, the Tin Woodsman, and the Lion their wishes? Did he do it or did they just think he did it?

3.   Make up a new adventure about one of Dorothy's friends, the Scarecrow with a brain, the Tin Woodsman with a heart, or the Lion who was now courageous.

4.   What do you think Dorothy did with her "magic" shoes?

5.   Do you think Dorothy will ever click her heels together three times and make another wish? Make up a new adventure about this.

Follow-Through Activities

•   Draw or paint Emerald City, showing the Wizard of Oz.

•   Rewrite the story. Let Dorothy and her friends go see the "man in the moon" or travel to Washington to see the president.

Stories Bibliography

All About Copy Kitten, Helen and Alf Evers. Rand McNally, 1940.

Alexander and the Terrible, Horrible, No Good, Very Bad Day, Judith Viorst. Atheneum, 1972.

Angus and the Cat, Marjorie Flack. Doubleday, 1931.

Amelia Bedelia, Peggy Parish. Harper & Row, 1983.

Babar Loses His Crown, Laurent de Brunhoff. Random House, 1967.

Curious George, Hans A. Rey. Houghton Mifflin, 1973.

Flip and the Cows, Dennis Wesley. Viking, 1942.

Frog and Toad Together, Arnold Lobel. Harper & Row, 1970.

Gilberto and the Wind, Marie Hall Ets. Viking, 1963.

Harry, the Dirty Dog, Gene Zion. Harper & Row, 1956.

Ira Sleeps Over, Bernard Waber. Houghton Mifflin, 1972.

Katy No-Pocket, Dennis Wesley. Viking 1942.

Lovable Lyle, Bernard Waber. Houghton Mifflin, 1969.

Make Way for Ducklings, Robert McCloskey. Viking, 1942.

No Roses for Harry, Gene Zion. Harper & Row, 1958.

A Pocket for Corduroy, Don Freeman. Viking Penguin, 1978.

The Sneetches, Dr. Seuss. Random House, 1961.

The Snowy Day, Ezra Jack Keats. Viking, 1963.

The Story of Ferdinand, Munro Leaf. Viking Press, 1936.

The Tale of Peter Rabbit, Beatrix Potter. Warne, 1989.

The Wizard of Oz, L. Frank Baum. Ballantine, 1980.

NOTES

NOTES

NOTES

NOTES